C.I.A.
Collect · Interpret · Apply
Unit of Study

4TH GRADE
VOLUME 4.2

Epic Fantasy
The Castle in the Attic

Sarah Collinge
with Bethany Robinson

Seattle, Washington
Portland, Oregon
Denver, Colorado
Vancouver, B.C.
Scottsdale, Arizona
Minneapolis, Minnesota

Peanut Butter Publishing
943 NE Boat Street
Seattle, Washington 98105
206-860-4900
www.peanutbutterpublishing.com

Table of Contents

Welcome to the C. I. A. Unit of Study for *The Castle in the Attic*

This unit of study was put together for the purpose of teaching students how to read longer, more complex text. Unfortunately, in classrooms where only basal readers are used, many students do not learn how to make the transition from picture books, to series books, to more complex chapter books. As a result, students struggle during independent reading. This unit of study will teach students the fundamental processes of reading text, specifically longer, more complex chapter books. It follows an approach described in its companion text, *Raising the Standards through Chapter Books: The C. I. A. Approach (available for purchase at https://readsidebyside.com/shop/).* I hope you enjoy guiding your students through the authentic work of expert readers!

The book *The Castle in the Attic*, by Elizabeth Winthrop, was chosen for its theme and genre. It connects well to the first unit in the C. I. A. series for fourth grade, *Shiloh*. In classrooms where the *Shiloh* unit of study has already been taught, students will recognize that, like *Shiloh*, *The Castle in the Attic* addresses the common theme of right and wrong, as the main character, William, does something he believes is right but eventually comes to regret. Both *Shiloh* and *The Castle in the Attic* show students that even good people make mistakes—what is important is that they recognize their mistakes and seek to make things right again.

The genre of *The Castle in the Attic* is epic fantasy. This genre was intentionally chosen for your grade level in order to expose students to the quest pattern found in all epic fantasy. You will need to be aware of some important characteristics of this genre before teaching this unit.

Epic fantasy is considered a complex story structure because it is comprised of two stories. One story takes place in the real world and has its own list of characters, problems, and events. The second story takes place in the fantastical world and also has its own list of characters, problems, and events. Therefore, students will need to monitor their comprehension of both of these plots.

I know you will love reading epic fantasy with your fourth-graders! *The Castle in the Attic* is a fun and engaging story that will get kids excited to learn about knights, castles, and the Middle Ages.

Before starting this unit of study with students, you will want to read and label a copy of the book *The Castle in the Attic,* to be used as a teacher guide. You will also want to acquire a class set of books for students to use during read aloud. Take time to get to know the scope and sequence, and input lessons into your plan book ahead of time.

At the back of this unit, you will find a vocabulary handbook. Please print a copy of this handbook for each student. It will be used almost daily and is an essential component of this unit of study.

If this is your first time teaching a C. I. A. unit, you will want to first familiarize yourself with the C. I. A. approach. You will then need to lay the groundwork for optimizing your success with this unit in your classroom by:

- Designating a read-aloud block in your daily schedule
- Setting up a meeting area
- Planning for turn and talk
- Preparing reader's notebooks
- Printing vocabulary handbooks
- Locating multiple copies of the text
- Inputing daily lessons into your plan book
- Preparing for assessment

Get to Know the C. I. A. Approach

This unit of study follows the C. I. A. approach to reading chapter books. The C. I. A. approach provides a simple instructional framework that is designed to help your students move from low-level comprehension to higher-level thinking. This framework provides the structure for the lessons in this unit, and also for the lessons in its companion book club teacher's guide *(available for purchase at https://readsidebyside.com/shop/)*. *The framework can then be transferred easily into self-selected, independent reading.*

The book *Raising the Standards through Chapter Books: The C. I. A. Approach* describes the C. I. A. approach in detail, as well as routines for its implementation. To achieve the best results from the C. I. A. units of study, you need to have the foundational knowledge provided in this companion text. I suggest studying this book before you begin teaching this unit. You will also find brief outlines throughout this unit that will give you an overview of each stage of the C. I. A. process.

The acronym C. I. A. stands for collect critical information, interpret the text, and apply to your life. Readers collect critical information in the first quadrant of the text, interpret this information in the second and third quadrants, and finally, in the fourth quadrant, consider how the author's message can be applied to one's life. To plan for this type of thinking, students begin by dividing the book, *The Castle in the Attic*, into four relatively equal parts. These divisions remind students to use the C. I. A. acronym to guide the type of thinking they do in each quadrant of the text. Check-stops at the end of each quadrant will serve as tools for monitoring comprehension.

All the lessons in this unit reflect the C. I. A. approach. You can help illustrate the steps in the approach by setting up a bulletin board in your classroom that communicates the thought processes that are emphasized in each quadrant of the text. Use the following samples and documents to guide you.

Collect 1/4
- Character
- Setting
- Problem
- Main Events

✓ Retell Summary ⁂ Read Side by Side

Interpret 2/4
- Key Repeated:
  - Words
  - Phrases
- Author's Craft
- Theme

✓ Line of Thinking ⁂ Read Side by Side

Interpret 3/4
- Evidence
- Turning Point
- Author's Message

✓ Turning Point Writing ⁂ Read Side by Side

Apply 4/4
- Author's Message
- Evaluation

✓ Synthesis Summary Reflection ⁂ Read Side by Side

An example of a C. I. A. bulletin board displayed above the classroom library
(posters available at readsidebyside.com/shop)

C	I	A
collect critical information	**interpret the text**	**apply to your life**

During this quadrant of text readers… • Name the important **characters** and infer character traits • Name and visualize the **setting** • Think about the **problem** and **important events** • Use comprehension strategies to **monitor** comprehension	**During this quadrant of the text readers…** • Use comprehension strategies to get to **deeper thinking** • Recognize key **repeated words/ phrases** • Start to think about possible **lines of thinking**	**During this quadrant of the text readers…** • Look for **evidence** to support a line of thinking	**During this quadrant of the text readers…** • Continue to look for **evidence** to support a line of thinking • Confirm and revise **predictions** • Think about **problem/ solution/results** • **Evaluate** how the author ties up all the loose ends • Consider how the book will impact his/her **life**
Readers read **slowly** and often **re-read.**	Readers **increase their speed** a little bit, and re-read less.	Readers **increase their speed** even more and rarely, if ever, re-read.	Readers **read without interruption** to the end.
At the end of the first quarter, readers **stop and summarize** in order to check comprehension and make sure they have the story in their head.	At the end of the 2nd quarter, readers **stop and name a line of thinking.**	At the end of the 3rd quarter, readers… • find the **turning-point** • consider how the turning-point reveals the **author's message** • **predict** how the book will end	At the end of the book, readers **confirm or reject their predictions** and **evaluate** the author's ending. Then readers reflect on their reading: • **summarize** • **synthesize** • **evaluate**

Visualize the Year

This unit is part of a series designed specifically for fourth-graders that includes five C. I. A. units and five corresponding book club units. Use the read-aloud units to supplement your current reading materials, or add the book club component to create a comprehensive English language arts curriculum.

Each series of C. I. A. units of study, one for each grade level from grade three through grade six, focuses on explicitly teaching a variety of genres over the course of the school year. The C. I. A. units for fourth grade cover complex genres appropriate for the grade level and expose students to themes, ideas, and knowledge sources that are foundational to the work they will be continuing through junior high and high school, thereby preparing students for increased text complexity in the upper grades. In addition, the units for fourth grade offer a social studies connection as students learn about westward expansion and the Yukon gold rush.

The suggested scope and sequence for fourth grade is as follows:

MONTHS	GENRE	TITLE & AUTHOR
September–October	Realistic Fiction	**READ-ALOUD** *Shiloh* Phyllis Reynolds Naylor
October–November	Realistic Fiction	**BOOK CLUBS** *Shoeshine Girl* Clyde Robert Bulla *Because of Winn-Dixie* Kate DiCamillo *How to Steal a Dog* Barbara O'Connor
October–November	Epic Fantasy	**READ-ALOUD** *The Castle in the Attic* Elizabeth Winthrop
November–December	Epic Fantasy	**BOOK CLUBS** *The Weeping Werewolf* Bruce Coville *The Dragonslayers* Bruce Coville *Into the Land of the Unicorns* Bruce Coville
January–February	Biography	**READ-ALOUD** *Streams to the River, River to the Sea* Scott O'Dell

February–March	Nonfiction	**BOOK CLUBS** *Going Along with Lewis & Clark* Barbara Fifer
March–April	Historical Nonfiction	**READ-ALOUD** *Children of the Gold Rush* Claire Rudolf Murphy & Jane G. Haigh
March–April	Historical Fiction	**BOOK CLUBS** *The Year of Miss Agnes* Kirkpatrick Hill *Riding Freedom* Pam Muñoz Ryan *The Sign of the Beaver* Elizabeth George Speare
April–May	Historical Fiction	**READ-ALOUD** *Aurore of the Yukon* Keith Halliday
May–June	Nonfiction	**BOOK CLUBS** *The Kids Book of Canada's Railway and How the CPR was Built* Deborah Hodge

(For more information about the fourth-grade scope and sequence, visit readsidebyside.com)

Each unit of study takes approximately six to eight weeks to complete and each book club unit takes approximately five to seven weeks to complete. This scope and sequence allows for some scheduling "wiggle room" to accommodate a variety of interruptions, including vacations and testing windows.

For the purpose of helping students make intertextual links, it is recommended that teachers read the books students have read in C. I. A. units of study in previous grades. Please check the website readsidebyside.com to see the scope and sequence of other grade levels.

Set Up for Success

In this section, I describe a number of ways in which you can facilitate the smoothest possible implementation of the lessons in this unit of study.

Prepare a Teacher's Guide

You will want to begin reading the book *The Castle in the Attic* on your own in preparation for teaching the lessons. Every read-aloud text you use in your classroom should be read by you ahead of time. It is always better to be prepared than surprised!

As you read the book, you may want to highlight and add labels to your teacher copy that will serve as additional references during your teaching of the lessons. While this is optional, I find that having these notes and highlights in my own copy of the text as I am reading aloud to students is very helpful. Instructions for highlighting the text can be found at the back of this unit. A black and white copy of the labels and directions for putting them into your book are also included at the back of this unit. Print the label sheet on clear full-sheet labels. I suggest using Avery #18665 labels or a comparable product. You will need to cut the labels before placing them in your teacher copy of *The Castle in the Attic*.

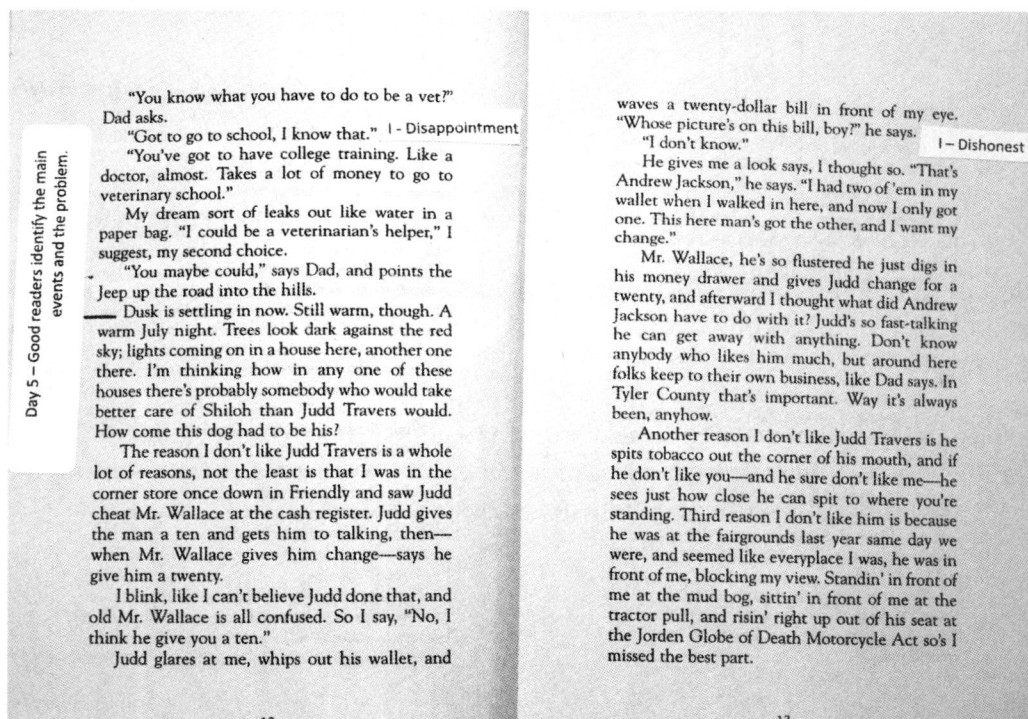

An example of a teacher book with labels

Designate a Daily Read-Aloud Block

"In the teaching of reading, there are only a handful of things that everyone agrees are essential. Perhaps the most important of these is the fact that children need to listen to the best of children's literature read aloud to them" (Calkins, 2001, p. 51).

The most coveted, protected time in a student's school day should be that in which he or she has the opportunity to listen and respond to quality literature that is at or above his or her grade level. This exposure to challenging levels of authentic literacy is critical to students' achievement (Schmoker, 2011). This C. I. A. unit is designed to be taught with *all* students in the room, including those who qualify for special services. Throughout this unit, I will refer to this time as the read-aloud block. (Please note: this block will *not* accommodate all of your necessary reading instruction. Critical elements of reading are not included in this unit and will have to be addressed during the school day outside of the read-aloud block.)

In some schools, students who receive special services are pulled for the entire reading block. In order to meet these students' needs, you will have to creatively find a time in the day when all students can be present for the instructional read-aloud. You will need a 45-minute stretch of time that is uninterrupted. Ideally, this block should be at the same time every day, throughout the entire school week.

Here is a sample fourth-grade block schedule that prioritizes reading:

- 8:55 Bell rings
- 9:00 **Read-Aloud Block**
- 9:45 **Book Club Block/Differentiated Instruction Block**
  (students might be pulled for reading intervention)
- 10:40 Plan Time Coverage
- 11:25 Math Block
- 12:20 Lunch
- 12:55 Math Workshop
- 2:00 Recess
- 2:15 Content Area Literacy (Social Studies, Science, Writing)
- 3:30 Dismiss

Prepare a Meeting Area

The "hub of the classroom" (Taberski, 2000, p. 21), the meeting area should be a comfortable place for students to gather in partnerships for reading, thinking about, and talking about books. The majority of the read-aloud block will be spent in this area; therefore, it needs to be a fairly large space conducive to learning.

A fourth-grade meeting space is usually defined by outlying furniture such as chairs, couches, or benches. A large rug creates a gathering place where students can sit crisscross. Students are assigned partnerships and places to sit, ensuring that the learning gets started quickly.

While cozy, the meeting area is not a place to relax; it's a place for rigorous learning. This is communicated to students through the positioning of the class easel, "the focal point of the meeting area" (Taberski, 2000, p. 21). Co-created charts are constructed daily on this easel and then moved to the bulletin board space on the walls to either side. Displaying these charts turns them into essential tools that students can use to monitor their comprehension while reading, extend their thinking, and transfer the processes learned in read-aloud into their small-group or independent reading time.

Fourth-graders sit in the meeting area, ready for the read-aloud to begin.

Get Ready for Turn and Talk

Every lesson throughout this unit of study is designed to gradually release students from teacher modeling to guided practice. Eventually, students will be conducting the work of expert readers independently in self-selected literature. In order for this to happen, students need to feel part of a safe community, in which every student has a voice. One of the best practices in the teaching of reading is that of giving students daily opportunities to talk in partnerships about their reading (Zemelman, Daniels, & Hyde, 2005).

Calkins tells teachers we should, "at every grade level (kindergarten through eighth grade) read books aloud and deliberately structure opportunities to talk about them, so that children learn to think, talk, and write thoughtfully in response to literature" (2001, p. 226). Assigning turn and talk partnerships that will last throughout the duration of the unit of study will help students examine their thinking and respond to each others' ideas. In addition, by building on what they talk about each day, partnerships will develop their thinking into big ideas or theories about literature.

Assign Partners

I recommend pairing students who are close in reading level, rather than having a struggling reader paired with an on-grade-level or above-grade-level reader. Once partnerships are formed, consider which student of each pair will need the most support. Highlight that student's name. This will be helpful in the next stage of implementing turn and talk.

Note: If you have an uneven number of students, create one trio. Place the student who is repeatedly absent or tardy in the trio. This will alleviate the stress of having to accommodate for that student's absences. Train students to join up with nearby partnerships when their regular partners are absent. This adjustment should be something students are responsible for on their own.

Prepare for Stems

Every lesson in this unit will use a turn and talk stem to encourage a high level of talk in your classroom. Not only will turn and talk support English language learners and struggling readers, it will also lift readers at the highest levels to a new standard of conversation. Angelillo tells us, "we must teach [students] how to talk about books and give them visions of what they can actually say" (2003, p. 18). Using the stems communicates how readers talk to one another authentically and trains students for this rigorous work.

To prepare for using the stems, create a poster that lists turn and talk partners. The more confident, higher-level reader in each partnership should be listed in the first column, and the less confident, more struggling reader should be listed in the second column. Ensure that each column is written in a different color. Initially, the students listed on the chart in the first column will be the starters, and students listed in the second column will be the responders. Roles will switch throughout the lesson; the struggling readers will always have a chance to hear their partners model the use of the stems before they are asked to take their turns.

This poster should be prominently displayed in your meeting area, to remind students whom they are responsible for sitting with, and what their roles in the partnerships will be.

Turn & Talk

Henry	Alex
Brisa	Michelle
Brock	Manny
Thanh	Jose A.
Cynthia	Aiyanna
Daphne	Octavia
Jose B.	Christian
Nicole	Vanessa
Chandler	Hassan
Katie	Haley
Wonderful	Cora
Hailey	Matthew Danell
Claire	Sarena
Tassya	Kathy

Sample turn and talk poster. Names in the left column are written in red. Names in the right column are written in blue. Sticky notes indicate which partnerships are assigned to the benches this week.

Create Stems

You will need a few materials to get you started using turn and talk stems:

- sentence strips
- a standard sentence-strip pocket chart
- markers
- clothespins or magnets in two colors
- a list of stems for this unit of study
- a storage box for holding sentence strips

To prepare for turn and talk, follow the steps below.

1. Write all turn and talk stems for this unit of study on sentence strips, including the following response stems:

   I agree/disagree with you because _____ .

   It sounds like you are saying_____ .

   I also think_____ .

2. Display these stems in your pocket chart as needed, and hang the chart in the meeting area.
3. Use clothespins or magnets to indicate which turn and talk partner is sharing or responding.
4. Store additional sentence strips in the storage box. Keep this in your meeting area.

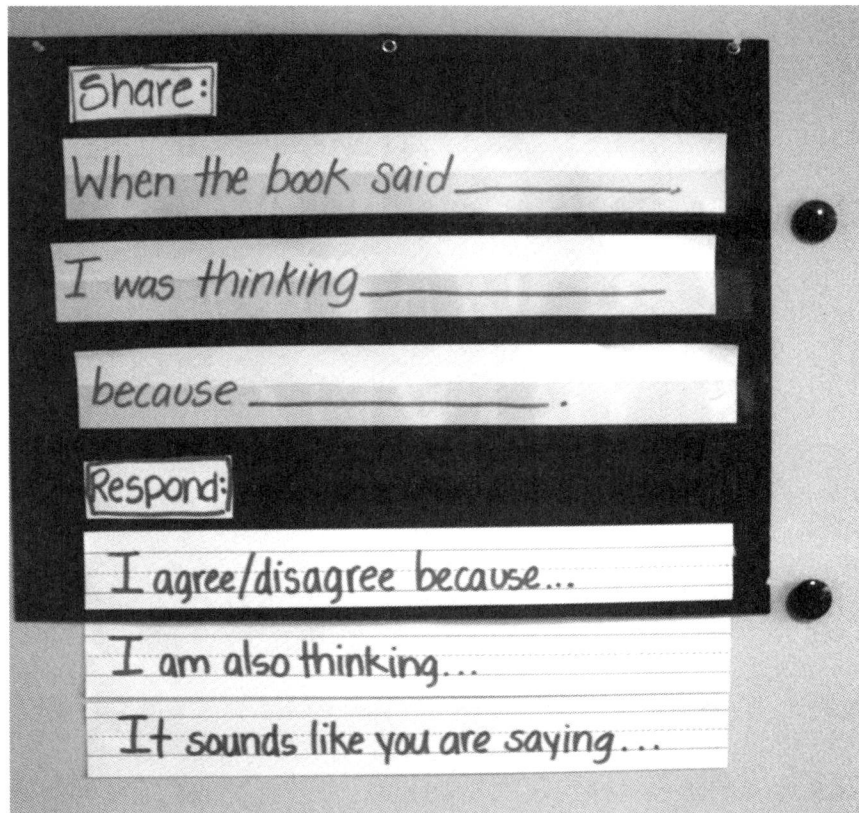

Sample stems chart with colored magnets to assign roles.

Prepare Reader's Notebooks

Just as writers keep notebooks to record ideas for writing, readers keep notebooks to record thoughts while reading (Buckner, 2009). Rather than a showcase of work, the reader's notebook is a tool for comprehension. This tool will be essential throughout this unit of study and will help students organize their thinking about the text in order to better understand its meaning.

I like to use the traditional composition books for my students' reader's notebooks because they are durable, a nice size, and easy to make more personal. Students will use approximately 20 pages for each read-aloud book. I recommend using durable tabs to mark sections of 20 pages. If the tabs are put in ahead of time, students can enter work on more than one book at a time without worrying about running out of pages in any one section.

Students can personalize their reader's notebooks by adding clip art, magazine clippings, personal art work, and stickers to the front and back covers. Cover the decorations with clear packing tape for durability.

Get Ready for Vocabulary Instruction

"Teacher read-aloud is one of the major opportunities for children to learn new word meanings" (Cunningham & Allington, 2007, p. 98). Therefore, vocabulary work will be an essential component of the read-aloud block.

Words selected for explicit instruction in this unit of study are words that appear over and over again or are inferred repeatedly throughout the text. Students expand their vocabulary knowledge when they are given the opportunity to learn synonyms and antonyms of key words.

Vocabulary will be reinforced through both turn and talk and writing. Students will be expected to practice using new vocabulary when they are talking in partnerships and writing in their notebooks. Teachers will reinforce the use of new vocabulary through dialogues with students. Vocabulary words taught in the read-aloud unit will be revisited during the paired book club unit.

At the back of this unit, you will find materials that can be copied to create vocabulary handbooks for students to use throughout this unit of study. (This vocabulary handbook is also available to download at readsidebyside.com.) Words will be introduced on the days indicated in the scope and sequence. On any given day, the vocabulary mini-lesson precedes the read-aloud, so that right after receiving instruction on a word, students have the opportunity to see the word used in the text and to use the word in their turn and talk. The following routine should be used for teaching vocabulary and should take up no more than 10 minutes of the read-aloud block.

Vocabulary Mini-Lesson Routine

1. Introduce the word and highlight morphemes.	*Today our target word is...* If applicable: *What is the root? (underline the root) What does the root mean? What is the prefix? (circle the prefix) What does the prefix mean? What is the suffix? (box the suffix) What does the suffix mean?*
2. Read the context(s) of the word. Highlight any clues that will help the reader infer the meaning.	*Our target word comes right from our text on page _____. Let's read it together. Are there any clues in the sentence that help us infer what this word means?*
3. Turn and talk: What does the word _____ mean?	*Based on the clues, what words or phrases describe this word? Turn and talk.*
4. Share-out and add to chart.	*What did you come up with?* *add accurate examples to the chart
5. Brainstorm other contexts for this word.	*In what other contexts might we find this word?* *add accurate examples to the chart
6. Turn and talk: What are opposites of this word?	*What words or phrases describe the opposite of this word? Turn and talk.*
7. Share-out and add to chart.	*What did you come up with?* *add accurate examples to the chart
8. I will remember this word...	*How will you remember this word? Draw a picture, or write a phrase that will help you remember this word. Use an example from your own life if possible.*
9. Link...	*Today and every day I want you to be looking for forms of this word in your reading. I also want you to practice using this word in your talk and in your writing.*

Locate Multiple Copies of the Text

By the time students reach intermediate grades, they are expected to be able to support their thinking with evidence pulled directly from text (Angelillo, 2003). How can students master this skill when the teacher is the only one holding a copy of the text? Document cameras are certainly one effective tool, but I want my students to practice flipping through pages, searching for evidence on their own. This is why I make it a priority to locate multiple copies of every book I read aloud and why I require students to follow along in their own copies of the text as I read aloud. Here are some suggestions for acquiring multiple copies without incurring a huge financial burden.

- Begin by searching through your own school library. Talk to the librarian. Sometimes there are class sets or multiple copies stored in other locations for teacher use only.
- Purchase used books from online resources that offer free shipping, such as www.thriftbooks.com, for example.
- Purchase new books at a discount at readsidebyside.com/shop/.
- Seek funding from your building budget, PTA, or outside sources such as DonorsChoose.org.

Input Daily Lessons Into Your Plan Book

I can't tell you how important it is to lay this unit out ahead of time. The more organized you are up front, the more successful you will feel, especially when trying something for the first time. Use the scope and sequence to get a feel for how long the unit will last, and be thoughtful about student holidays, especially longer breaks like winter break and spring break. You wouldn't want to send your students off for the winter holiday with only three chapters left to read in the read-aloud book!

Be mindful of any interruptions to your read-aloud block. Daily lessons will consume the entire 45 minutes. Any interruptions, even small, could throw off the calendar.

Don't get started with this unit until you have established basic routines in your classroom. I like to teach a few management mini-lessons before launching into the unit. At the beginning of a school year, you might give yourself a week or two before starting your first read-aloud unit of study. Always hold high expectations for management. You don't want precious instructional time to be lost due to management failures!

Use the scope and sequence to help you place daily lessons in your plan book.

Prepare for Assessment

Throughout this unit of study, you will have many opportunities to practice ongoing, informal assessment of your students.

One of the key ways in which you will gather information about your students' growth is by listening in on their turn and talk conversations. Create a system for listening in to various conversations each day. Simply check off partnerships as you visit them to ensure that you listen to all partnerships several times during the unit. I suggest observing each partnership twice in quadrant one, once in quadrant two, and one more time in quadrant three. This would allow you to compare conversations between partners over the course of the unit. Try to remain in the role of either observer or coach when listening in on partnerships. It's important that you do not take over the conversations or do the students' work for them.

Your observations during turn and talk time will give you information about your students' levels of listening comprehension. You will be able to observe many important things during turn and talk time. I encourage you to take notes as you observe, or you can record conversations on a voice recorder and then play them back later and log your notes at that time. You can download an observation check sheet from readsidebyside.com, or purchase observation check sheet notepads at shop. readsidebyside.com. This simple check sheet will be useful for recording your observations of

1. The quality of reciprocal conversations between partners (speaking and listening standards).
2. The level of thinking students are exhibiting, be it explicit thinking, inferential thinking, the drawing of deeper conclusions, or evaluation of the text (reading standards).
3. References to evidence in the text and from outside sources (reading standards).
4. Use of key vocabulary (language standards).

The reader's notebook will also be a place to find evidence of student learning. The charts in the reader's notebook will usually be made in guided practice; however, the informal writing pieces students do throughout the unit, if done independently, provide good opportunities to see if students have met the learning targets. The informal writing pieces students do throughout the unit, if done independently, provide good opportunities to see if students have met the learning targets.

Grading reader's notebooks can become overwhelming, especially when you end up carrying them all home over a weekend. I have had great success using suggestions offered by Mike Schmoker in his online article *Write More, Grade Less* (1996). In line with his recommendations, students will be writing short, informal compositions in their reader's notebooks. Each piece will focus on a specific, explicitly taught skill or strategy. When the writing assignments are kept short and informal, students gain more practice and therefore are more successful.

As students are working on these short writing pieces, I wander the room, grading student work as I go. The students are alongside me as I grade their work, offering the opportunity for them to self-evaluate. In addition, students are allowed to make changes to their work with my help. I simply mark in the margin whether the work was completed independently or with guidance. This immediate feedback is critical to student improvement and allows all students to engage in dialogue about what grade-level-standard writing looks like. They can instantly see where they can improve as both readers and writers and can then set goals toward that improvement.

The same writing frames used in this unit of study are taught in all C. I. A. units of study that are part of the yearlong sequence. Therefore, over time, I can lay a series of writing pieces out in front of me when grading and see how a student has made progress across a trimester or throughout the course of a school year. Focusing on student growth provides a more meaningful picture of progress than does a one-time grade and also allows me to use more than one piece of evidence to determine whether a learning target has been met.

The check sheets and rubrics available on the Read Side by Side website have been designed to make it easier for you to collect evidence of student progress relative to grade-level standards over time. These tools facilitate the grading of both writing skills and reading comprehension.

While grading student entries, it is important to remember that all notebook entries should be well organized and easy to read. If the reader's notebook is going to be used as a tool for comprehension, then students should be able to easily find and read pages in their notebooks. I find that fourth-grade students are still motivated by stickers and smiley faces. Use these motivators to encourage neat work.

Alignment to the Common Core State Standards

All lessons in this unit of study are aligned to our nation's Common Core State Standards (Common Core State Standards Initiative [CCSSI], 2010). At the beginning of each lesson, you will see an outline of the learning targets for that particular day. The following abbreviations are used to link these targets to the Common Core State Standards:

RL	Reading Standards for Literature
RI	Reading Standards for Informational Text
W	Writing Standards
SL	Speaking and Listening Standards
L	Language Standards

The yearlong series of C. I. A. read-aloud units, partnered with the C. I. A. Book Club Teacher's Guides, provide a comprehensive English language arts curriculum for grades 3—6. All C. I. A. read-aloud and book club units are available at readsidebyside.com/shop/. These units expose students to grade-level and above standards, in text that is matched to the complexity bands of the Common Core State Standards.

To download a copy of the Common Core State Standards, visit http://www.corestandards.org/the-standards.

To download a copy of the vertical progressions of the Common Core State Standards, and additional Common Core resources, visit readsidebyside.com.

Distribution of Common Core State Standards, C. I. A. Unit of Study Epic Fantasy, *The Castle in the Attic, The Castle in the Attic 4.2*

Reading Standards for Literature (RL)

Days	1	2	3	4	5	6	7	8	9	10	11	12	13	14	15	16	17	18	19	20	21	22	23	24	25	26	27	28	29	30	31	32	33-38
Key Ideas and Details																																	
#1 Read closely / Monitor comprehension / Support thinking	X	X	X	X		X	X	X	X		X	X		X		X	X		X		X	X	X	X	X	X	X	X	X	X	X		
#2 Determine theme / Author's message / Summarize the text										X	X									X	X	X	X	X		X	X		X		X	X	
#3 Analyze story elements	X	X	X	X		X	X	X	X	X	X	X		X	X	X	X		X				X		X		X	X					
Craft and Structure																																	
#4 Recognize author's craft / Recognize intertextuality						X					X											X						X					
#5 Analyze text structure / Infer genre / Compare multiple genres	X		X	X		X	X	X			X	X					X		X	X			X		X		X	X	X	X			
#6 Recognize point of view / Compare point of view / Author's perspective														X	X							X						X	X	X	X		
Integration of Knowledge																																	
#7 Connect to other representations of the topic (visual, oral)																																	
#8 (Not applicable to literature)																																	
#9 Compare and contrast themes across 1 genre															X					X				X									

By the end of the year, read and comprehend literature in the grades 4–5 text complexity band proficiently, with scaffolding as needed.

Distribution of Common Core State Standards, C. I. A. Unit of Study Epic Fantasy, *The Castle in the Attic* 4.2

Reading Standards for Informational Text (RI)

Days	1	2	3	4	5	6	7	8	9	10	11	12	13	14	15	16	17	18	19	20	21	22	23	24	25	26	27	28	29	30	31	32	33–38
Key Ideas and Details																																	
#1 Read closely / Monitor comprehension / Support thinking					X													X															
#2 Main idea and details / Summarize the text					X													X															
#3 Sequence of events / Cause and effect					X													X															
Craft and Structure																																	
#4 Recognize author's craft																																	
#5 Analyze text structure: Compare/Contrast Problem/Solution Cause/Effect																																	
#6 Recognize point of view / Compare point of view / Author's perspective					X																												
Integration of Knowledge																																	
#7 Connect to other representations of the topic (visual, oral)					X													X															
#8 Explain author's use of reasons and evidence to make a point																																	
#9 Integrate text on 1 topic					X													X															

By the end of the year, read and comprehend informational text in the grades 4–5 text complexity band proficiently, with scaffolding as needed.

Language Standards (L)

Days	1	2	3	4	5	6	7	8	9	10	11	12	13	14	15	16	17	18	19	20	21	22	23	24	25	26	27	28	29	30	31	32	33-38
Conventions of Standard English																																	
#1 English grammar and usage	Not explicitly taught in this unit of study. Students are expected to use proper English grammar and usage when writing and speaking in this unit. Supplement the unit with grammar and usage lessons as needed.																																
#2 English capitalization, punctuation, and spelling	Not explicitly taught in this unit of study. Students are expected to use proper English capitalization, punctuation and spelling when writing. Supplement the unit with these lessons as needed.																																
Knowledge of Language																																	
#3 Convey ideas precisely / Use formal English when appropriate	X	X	X	X	X	X	X	X	X	X	X	X	X	X	X	X	X	X	X	X	X	X	X	X	X	X	X	X	X	X	X	X	X
Vocabulary Acquisition and Use																																	
#4 Monitor meaning of unknown words: Context, Morphemes, Reference materials	X	X	X	X		X	X	X			X	X	X			X	X	X	X		X	X	X	X	X	X	X	X		X			X
#5 Figurative language, Word relationships, Idioms, adages, proverbs, Synonyms, Antonyms	X	X	X	X		X	X	X			X	X	X			X	X				X	X	X	X	X	X	X	X	X	X			X
#6 Acquire and use grade-appropriate vocabulary in speaking and writing	X	X	X	X	X	X	X	X	X	X	X	X	X	X	X	X	X	X	X	X	X	X	X	X	X	X	X	X	X	X	X	X	X

Speaking and Listening Standards (SL)

Days	1	2	3	4	5	6	7	8	9	10	11	12	13	14	15	16	17	18	19	20	21	22	23	24	25	26	27	28	29	30	31	32	33-38
Comprehension and Collaboration																																	
#1 Express ideas clearly / Build on other's ideas / Respond to questions / Summarize discussions	X	X	X	X	X	X	X	X	X	X	X	X	X	X	X	X	X	X	X	X	X	X	X	X	X	X	X	X	X	X	X	X	X
#2 Paraphrase after listening to text read aloud / Paraphrase after listening to a presentation	X	X	X	X	X	X	X	X	X	X	X	X	X	X	X	X	X	X	X	X	X	X	X	X	X	X	X	X	X	X	X	X	
#3 Identify reasons and evidence given by a speaker																																	
Presentation of Knowledge and Ideas																																	
#4 Speak clearly / Speak with a good pace	X	X	X	X	X	X	X	X	X	X	X	X	X	X	X	X	X	X	X	X	X	X	X	X	X	X	X	X	X	X	X	X	X
#5 Present with media support					X	X	X	X	X	X	X	X	X	X	X	X			X	X	X	X	X	X	X								
#6 Use formal English when appropriate to the task	X	X	X	X	X	X	X	X	X	X	X	X	X	X	X	X	X	X	X	X	X	X	X	X	X	X	X	X	X	X	X	X	X

Distribution of Common Core State Standards, C. I. A. Unit of Study Epic Fantasy, *The Castle in the Attic 4.2*

Writing Standards (W)

Days	1	2	3	4	5	6	7	8	9	10	11	12	13	14	15	16	17	18	19	20	21	22	23	24	25	26	27	28	29	30	31	32	33-38
Text Types and Purposes																																	
#1 Write an opinion piece																													X				
#2 Write an expository piece										X					X																	X	X
#3 Write a narrative piece																																	
Production and Distribution of Writing																																	
#4 Written clearly, Appropriate organization, Task, purpose, and audience considered										X					X														X			X	X
#5 Strengthen writing through the stages of the writing process																																	X
#6 Produce and publish writing using technology																																	X
Research to Build and Present Knowledge																																	
#7 Investigate different aspects of 1 topic	X		X	X	X																												
#8 Recall information, Gather information, Take notes/categorize			X		X		X	X		X			X	X	X	X	X			X	X		X	X		X	X	X	X			X	X
#9 Draw evidence							X	X		X					X					X	X			X		X		X	X			X	X
Range of Writing																																	
#10 Extended time frame																													X				X
#10 Short time frame										X					X																	X	

The Castle in the Attic Text Complexity

QUALITATIVE MEASURES	QUANTITATIVE MEASURES
Levels of Meaning The text offers multiple levels of meaning and nuances of abstract concepts related to right and wrong, and good and evil. In addition, the author tells a coming-of-age story, revealing the qualities that prove young adulthood. Critical vocabulary important to the theme is inferred in the text. **Structure** Epic fantasy follows a complex story structure in which there are multiple plots including a real-world and a fantastical-world plot. Readers must infer how these two plots relate to one another and communicate a common theme. **Language Conventionality and Clarity** Elizabeth Winthrop uses language that is fairly literal and clear. Challenges emerge through use of dialect and uncommon vocabulary and through an unconventional use of grammar in dialogue. **Knowledge Demands** General background knowledge about the Middle Ages, knights, kings, and castles is needed to comprehend this text. In addition, readers will make connections to classic stories of King Arthur. Throughout the text there are references to the Code of Chivalry, and there are some biblical references as well.	The Lexile level for *The Castle in the Attic* is 750 based on word frequency and sentence length. This is in the early range of the complexity band for 4th–5th grade according to the Common Core State Standards. **READER TASK CONSIDERATIONS** These should be determined locally with reference to motivation, knowledge, and experiences as well as to purpose and the complexity of the tasks assigned and the questions posed.

The Castle in the Attic Scope and Sequence

NOTE: The lessons for this unit give page references for the 1985 Yearling publication.

Unit of Study: *The Castle in the Attic*   **Genre: Epic Fantasy**

DAY	CHAPTER(S)/ PAGES	MINI-LESSON	READ-ALOUD
1	Blurb	**Vocabulary:** *quest* Use sticky notes to mark each quadrant of the text.	Search for key story elements in the blurb. • Complete story elements handout together • Identify genre • Make a prediction
2		**Vocabulary:** *hero* **vs.** *villain* Use the genre chart to help students understand what to expect from epic fantasy.	
3	Chapter 1 pp. 3–7	**Vocabulary:** *deceitful*	Focus on using comprehension strategies to determine important characters and infer character traits. • Co-create a character list
4	Chapter 2 pp. 8–12	**Vocabulary:** *chivalry*	Focus on the setting. • Use the castle diagram to "walk through the castle"
5	Outside Text: *The Legend of King Arthur*		Focus on what makes King Arthur an important person to know about.
6	Chapter 2 pp. 12–16	**Vocabulary:** *tradition*	Recognize the author's craft of foreshadowing and use the big clues generated by this technique to make predictions.
7	Chapter 3 pp. 17–25	**Vocabulary:** *friend* **vs.** *foe*	Focus on important details in order to visualize characters. • Continue to co-create a character list

DAY	CHAPTER(S)/ PAGES	MINI-LESSON	READ-ALOUD
8	Chapter 4 pp. 26–31	**Vocabulary:** *power*	Focus on important story elements. • Character list
9	Chapter 4 pp. 31–40		Focus on the important events. • Co-create an important events list (Sir Simon's story)
10		Retell summary writing and share-out. • Sir Simon's story	
11	Chapter 5 pp. 41–48	**Vocabulary:** *legend*	Consider what is right and what is wrong.
12	Chapter 6 pp. 49–56	**Vocabulary:** *freedom* vs. *tyranny*	Focus on important information and use that information to make predictions. • Co-create a list of predictions
13	Chapter 7 pp. 57–62	**Vocabulary:** *unwilling*	Identify the problem and solution. • Co-create a problems list

DAY	CHAPTER(S)/ PAGES	MINI-LESSON	READ-ALOUD
14	Chapter 7 pp. 62–70	(After read-aloud) Consider the function of time in epic fantasy.	Consider how two characters are similar and different. • Co-create a comparison chart
15		Comparison writing • William vs. Alastor	
16	Chapter 8 pp. 71–77	Vocabulary: disapproval	Focus on inferring a character's feelings. • Continue to co-create a problems list
17	Chapter 9 pp. 78–87	Vocabulary: regret	Focus on inferring the main character's feelings and motivations. • Continue to co-create a problems list

DAY	CHAPTER(S)/ PAGES	MINI-LESSON	READ-ALOUD
18	Outside Text: Becoming a Knight		Consider how events are similar and different and use those events to make predictions.
19	Chapter 9 pp. 87–92	**Vocabulary:** *peace offering*	Focus on using knowledge of the genre to make predictions.
20		Focus on naming a line of thinking. • Co-create an evidence collection box	
21	Chapter 10 pp. 93–101	**Vocabulary:** *mercy*	Focus on important events and add evidence to support a line of thinking. • Continue to co-create an evidence collection box
22	Chapter 10 pp. 102–107	**Vocabulary:** *knight*	Consider the purpose of multiple plots.

DAY	CHAPTER(S)/ PAGES	MINI-LESSON	READ-ALOUD
23	Chapter 11 pp. 108–111	**Vocabulary:** *tempted*	Visualize the setting. • Co-create a setting map
24	Chapter 11 pp. 111–116	**Vocabulary:** *apparition*	Collect evidence to support a line of thinking. • Continue to co-create an evidence collection box
25	Chapters 11 & 12 pp. 116–121	**Vocabulary:** *steadfast*	Focus on the relationships of events (cause and effect).
26	Chapter 12 pp. 121–128	**Vocabulary:** *compassionate*	Collect evidence to support a line of thinking. • Continue to co-create an evidence collection box • Continue to co-create a setting map
27	Chapter 12 pp. 128–130	**Vocabulary:** *foolish* **vs.** *wise*	Focus on keeping track of important characters. • Co-create a fantastical-world character list
28	Chapter 13 pp. 131–139	**Vocabulary:** *courage*	Infer the most important event in the story—the turning point— and use that event to infer the author's message. • Continue to co-create an evidence collection box
29		Turning point writing and share-out.	
30	Chapter 14 pp. 140–148	**Vocabulary:** *imprisoned* **vs.** *freed*	Use the turning point to predict how the story will end.

DAY	CHAPTER(S)/ PAGES	MINI-LESSON	READ-ALOUD
31	Read-In Chapters 15–17 pp. 149–179		
32		Synthesis summary	
33–38		Formal writing: Literary Essay Prove how the Code of Chivalry helped William overcome tests and prove his goodness. Describe how the Code of Chivalry has helped you overcome tests in your own life.	

The Castle in the Attic Stems List

Day 1 – Blurb
When the blurb said _____, I was thinking _____. This helps me understand _____ .

Day 2 – Genre
When the chart said _____, I made a prediction. I think _____ because_____ .

Day 3 – Character List
When the book said _____, I thought this was an important detail because_____ .

Day 4 – Setting
When the book said _____, I thought this was an important detail because_____ .

Day 5 – Outside Text
When the legend said _____, I thought this was an important detail. This shows that _____ is an important person because_____ .

Day 6 – Use Foreshadowing to Make Predictions
When the book said _____, I made a prediction. I was thinking_____ .

Day 7 –Character List
When the book said_____, I thought this was an important detail because _____ .

Day 8 – Infer Character Traits
When the book said _____, I was thinking _____ because _____ .

Day 9 – Important Events
When the book said _____, I was thinking this was important because _____ .

Day 11 – Right vs. Wrong
When the book said _____, I was thinking _____. I think it is right/wrong to _____ .

Day 12 – Use Important Information to Make Predictions
When the book said _____, I made a prediction. I was thinking_____ .

Day 13 – Problem and Solution
When the book said _____, I was thinking this was important because _____ .

Day 14 – Comparing and Contrasting Characters
When the book said _____, I was thinking _____ and _____ are alike/different because_____ .
This makes me think _____ .

Day 15 – Comparison Writing
I think William and Alastor are more alike/different because _____. Also because_____ .

Day 16 – Infer Characters' Feelings
When the book said _____, I was thinking _____ because _____. This helps me understand_____ .

The Castle in the Attic Unit of Study

Day 17 – Infer Characters' Feelings and Motivations
When the book said _____, I was thinking _____. This helps me understand_____ .

Day 18 – Outside Text
When the article said _____, I thought this was an important detail. This reminds me of _____
because_____ .

Day 19 – Make Predictions
When the book said _____, I made a prediction. I was thinking_____ .

Day 20 – Line of Thinking
I think the author is teaching me _____ because _____ .

Day 21 – Collect Evidence
When the book said _____, this supported my line of thinking. William followed the Code of
Chivalry when he _____. This proves he is _____ .

Day 22 – Purpose of Multiple Plots
When the book said _____, I thought this was important because _____. I think the author wants
me to know _____ .

Day 23 – Setting Map
When the book said _____, I thought this was an important detail because _____. This makes me
think _____ .

Day 24 – Collect Evidence
When the book said _____, this supported my line of thinking. William followed the Code of
Chivalry when he _____. This proves he is _____ .

Day 25 – Cause and Effect
When the book said _____, I thought this was a consequence of_____ .
This makes me think _____ .

Day 26 – Collect Evidence
When the book said _____, this supported my line of thinking. William followed the Code of
Chivalry when he _____. This proves he is _____ .

Day 27 – Character List
When the book said _____, I thought this was an important detail because_____ .

Day 28 – Turning Point
When the book said _____, I was thinking this was an important event because _____ .
This makes me think _____ .

Day 30 – Use the Turning Point to Make Predictions
When the book said _____, I made a prediction. I was thinking_____ .

Day 31 – Read-in
When the book said _____, I was thinking _____ because _____ .

Suggestions for Supporting Guided Practice

As you listen in on turn and talk conversations, use the outline below to help you decide when to:
- Provide a scaffold
- Return to teacher modeling
- Provide coaching
- Stretch students' conversations

Scenario #1
Observation:
The student is having trouble with the first part of the stem, "When the book said..."

Instructional Decision: Provide a scaffold.
Fill in the first part of the stem for the student, and release the second half of the stem back to the student.

Scenario #2
Observation:
Even after having the first part of the stem filled in, the student still struggles to use the second half of the stem.

Instructional Decision: Return to teacher modeling.
Stop student turn and talk. Provide teacher modeling for this student.

Scenario #3
Observation:
The student's thinking is inaccurate or not supported by textual evidence.

Instructional Decision: Encourage/provide coaching.
Encourage the other partner to respond to the first partner's thinking. Step in and ask a question when needed to guide the partners back on course.

Scenario #4
Observation:
The student accurately uses the stem and shows mastery of the strategy.

Instructional Decision: Stretch the conversation.
Take student thinking one level higher on Bloom's Taxonomy.

If the whole class requires any of the above types of support, interrupt turn and talk in order to provide the needed instruction or coaching.

C. I. A.
Lesson Plans

The Castle in the Attic

NOTE: The lessons for this unit give page references for the 1985 Yearling publication.

C
Collect Critical Information

Identify the main story elements:
- Character
- Setting
- Problem
- Main Events

In this quadrant, readers read slowly and often reread in order to monitor their comprehension.

After finishing this quadrant of the text, readers stop to check their understanding. They write a retell summary of the first quadrant of the book, including all the main story elements: character, setting, problem, and main events.

Days 1–10, Chapters 1–4

Mini-Lesson

Vocabulary Routine: *quest* (L 4, 5)
The Latin root 'quest' means *to seek or to ask.*

Instructional Read-Aloud

In this blurb...students will learn that William's housekeeper is leaving and that as a good-bye present she is giving him a model of a castle that is very lifelike. When William picks up the knight that goes with the castle, the knight comes to life. William goes on a fantastic quest to another land and time.

In this lesson...you will be modeling for students how you use clues in the blurb to help you get main elements of the story—character, setting, problem, and main events—in your head. After identifying these story elements, students will use them to make a prediction.

Learning Targets:

Read closely to monitor comprehension (RL 1)
- Make predictions

Show understanding of story elements (RL 3)
- Main characters
- Setting
- Problem

Infer genre (RL 5)

Gather and categorize information through note taking (W 8)

Convey ideas precisely using appropriate vocabulary (L 3, 6)

Engage in collaborative discussion (SL 1, 2, 4, 6)

Connect:

We have been learning...
...that good readers preview the book before they read to help them form ideas about the text and to set a purpose for reading.

Teach:

Today I am going to teach you...

...that good readers look carefully at the cover of a book and read the blurb prior to starting the first chapter so that they can begin to think about the story elements. The main elements of the story are character, setting, problem, and main events.

We are going to create the first entry in your notebooks today. I have copied a handout for you. We will be completing the handout together before gluing or taping your copies of the handout into your reader's notebooks. This entry will be a tool that we will use while reading this book; it will help us remember the most important story elements so that we can keep the story in our heads.

Today we will be using this stem for turn and talk:
When the blurb said _____, I was thinking _____. This helps me understand _____.

Listen and follow along while I read the blurb.
Read the entire blurb aloud.

Model:

As I read the blurb, I noticed the names of important characters. To help me remember these important characters as I read, I am going to add these names to my handout. I will also add any important information I have learned about each of the characters.

When the blurb said that William received the best present of his life, **I was thinking** that William is probably going to be the main character in the book. **This helps me understand** that William is going to be important to the plot.

Let's record William on the handout as the main character in our story.

(Model adding William to the handout.)

Guided Practice:

Who are the other important characters?

Turn and talk to your partners using this stem:
When the blurb said _____, I was thinking _____. This helps me understand _____.

(Model adding new characters to the handout.)

Model:

Now let's think about what information we found in the blurb about the setting.

When the blurb said "William is off on a fantastic quest to another land and another time," **I was thinking** that the book probably takes place in both a real world and an imaginary world. **This helps me understand** that the story is going to be a fantasy.

(Model adding this information to the handout.)

Guided Practice:

Did you learn any other important details about the setting?

Turn and talk to your partners using this stem:
When the blurb said _____, I was thinking _____. This helps me understand _____.

(Model adding new setting details to the handout.)

Guided Practice:

We can also use the blurb and the cover to identify the problem in the story.
What do you think the problem is in this story?

Turn and talk to your partners using this stem:
When the blurb said _____, I was thinking _____. This helps me understand _____.

(Model adding the problem to the handout.)

Guided Practice:

Good readers not only gather key information about the character, setting, and problem before reading, they also make predictions to help set a purpose for reading. Good readers use story elements and what they know about the genre to help them make predictions.

Write a prediction you can make about the story on your handout. Then, turn to your partner and share your prediction. Remember to share evidence of your thinking.

Link:

Today and every day when you read…
…I want you to think about the story elements before you start reading the first chapter, by paying close attention to the cover of the book and the information in the blurb. You can also use that information to help you make predictions.

Notebook Entry #1: Finding Story Elements in the Blurb

Before reading, good readers get the story in their head by reading the blurb and identifying story elements.

Blurb (Yearling, 1985):

William has just received the best present of his life. It's an old, real-looking stone and wooden model of a castle, with a drawbridge, a moat, and a finger-high knight to guard the gates. It's the mysterious castle his housekeeper has told him about, and even though William is sad she's leaving, now the castle is his!

William can't wait to play with it—he's certain there's something magical about the castle. And sure enough, when he picks up the tiny silver knight, it comes alive in his hand!

Sir Simon tells William a mighty story of wild sorcery, wizards, and magic. And suddenly William is off on a fantastic quest to another land and another time—where a fiery dragon and an evil wizard are waiting to do battle...

Characters:

Setting (place):

Setting (time):

Problem:

Prediction:

Mini-Lesson

In this lesson…you will model how readers break a long text into manageable pieces by dividing the text into quadrants. Marking each quadrant will help students set goals as they read.

Learning Target:

Analyze the structure of texts (RL 5)
- how larger portions of the text relate to each other and the whole

Connect:

We have been learning…
…that good readers get ready to read by looking at the blurb in order to pull out the most important story elements: character, setting, and plot.

Teach:

Today I am also going to teach you…
…that good readers, before reading, divide a book into four relatively equal quadrants. Good readers use various specific strategies to help them understand the text, depending on which quadrant they are reading in. They also use these divisions to help set their reading goals.

You will need three small sticky notes, preferably in different colors.

Quest
Hero
Villan
deceitful
Chivalry

Model:

First, open up your book to the last page. There are 179 pages in our book, *The Castle in the Attic.* If we take that number and divide it by 4, we get 45. We are going to divide our book into four quadrants that are each roughly 45 pages long. When marking quadrants, always make sure you end a quadrant at the end of a chapter.

Please place your first sticky note on page 40, at the end of chapter 4. In the first quadrant of the book we will be collecting story elements. We will stop at the end of this quadrant to write a retell summary as a way of monitoring our comprehension while reading.

Place your second sticky note on page 92. When we reach this page, we should have a big idea of what this book is going to be about. Therefore, in this second quadrant we will focus on understanding the genre and looking for patterns in our thinking.

Place your third sticky note on page 139. When we reach this page, we will have found the turning point of the book. The turning point is where the author's message is revealed. Therefore, in the third quadrant we will be collecting evidence to support our thinking about the story's theme.

In the last quadrant of the book, we will be rejecting or confirming predictions and evaluating how the author ties everything up at the end. In addition, we will be considering whether the author's message is one we agree with and can apply to our own lives.

Link:

Today and every day when you read…
…I want you to think about dividing the text into four quadrants in order to help focus your thinking and set goals for reading.

Mini-Lesson

Vocabulary Routine: *hero* vs. *villain* (L 4, 5)

Learning Targets:

Read closely to monitor comprehension (RL 1)

Show understanding of story elements (RL 3)

Use what you know about genre to help you understand the story better and compare texts (RL 5)
- Realistic fiction

Convey ideas precisely using appropriate vocabulary (L 3, 6)

Engage in collaborative discussion (SL 1, 2, 4, 6)

Connect:

We have been learning…
…that good readers think about story elements before they read by looking carefully at the cover and reading the blurb.

Teach:

Today I am going to teach you…
…that good readers also use what they know about the genre to think about character, setting, and plot. Knowledge of character, setting, and plot will be useful as you make predictions about the story. Today we are going to review the genre epic fantasy, which is the genre of *The Castle in the Attic*. We will be using the chart I have posted in our meeting area to help us think about this genre.

Notice how I use the information on this chart to help me make predictions about the book *The Castle in the Attic*.

Today we will be using this stem for turn and talk:
When the chart said _____, I made a prediction. I think _____ because _____.

Model:

When reading epic fantasy, you can expect characters to be fictional. Some of the characters may be fantastical, meaning that they could not exist in real life. Just as in realistic fiction, you can expect the main character in epic fantasy to change over time. The main character is a good and moral person who may prove to be the unexpected hero.

When the chart said that the main character in epic fantasy books changes over time, **I made a prediction. I think** William might change throughout the story **because** he is the main character in this book. I think he will be the unexpected hero of the story.

Guided Practice:

When reading epic fantasy, you can expect the story to occur in a fantastical place, either a real place with fantastical elements or in a fantastical world with realistic elements. Time is relatively unimportant or nonexistent.

Turn and talk to your partners using this stem:
When the chart said _____, I made a prediction. I think _____ because _____.

Guided Practice:

In epic fantasy, the main character changes over time. There is tension between good and bad, right and wrong. A quest pattern in often found in this genre.

Turn and talk to your partners using this stem:
When the chart said _____, I made a prediction. I think _____ because _____.

Model:

When reading epic fantasy, the most important element to focus on is the main character. You can expect to think about how the character changes over time. You can also expect to think about themes that are common throughout all epic fantasy, themes such as good vs. evil, and heroism.

Link:

Today and every day when you read…
…I want you to think about the genre of the book and use what you know about the genre to make predictions.

Genre Chart: Epic Fantasy

	Epic Fantasy
Setting	A fantastical place. • A realistic world with fantastical elements • A fantastical world with realistic elements Time is relatively unimportant or nonexistent
Characters	Fictional characters who are not necessarily believable. A main character who changes over time. The main character is a good or moral person. An unexpected hero is revealed.
Plot	The main character changes over time. There is tension between good and bad, right and wrong. A quest pattern is often found in this genre.
Most important story element	Character
Readers will think about	How does the main character change over time? How does the main character overcome challenges? What are the main character's beliefs about right and wrong?

Quest Pattern:
1. A precious object must be found and possessed.
2. The hero begins a long journey to find it.
3. A series of tests reveals the hero.
4. Guardians test the hero, and helpers assist the hero.
5. Good overcomes evil.

The Castle in the Attic Unit of Study

Mini-Lesson

Vocabulary Routine: *deceitful* (L 4, 5)
The base word deceit means *an attempt to trick.* The suffix 'ful' means *full of.*

Instructional Read-Aloud

In this chapter…you read that Mrs. Phillips, who has been William's nanny for ten years, will be leaving him. She will be returning to her home in England, where her brother lives. Mrs. Phillips has chosen to leave because she believes William is old enough to take care of himself. William desperately wants her to stay, and he decides to steal her prized possessions in hopes that she won't leave without them. At the end of the chapter, William gives these possessions back to Mrs. Phillips, and she tells him that she has a big surprise for him.

In this lesson…you will be modeling how readers keep track of important characters while reading and infer character traits. You will demonstrate how readers keep track of characters while reading by working with your students to co-create a character list that can be used as a tool for comprehension monitoring.

Learning Targets:

Read closely to monitor comprehension (RL 1)
- Infer character traits
- Visualize

Show understanding of story elements (RL 3)
- Character traits

Use what you know about genre to help you understand the story better (RL 5)

Gather and categorize information through note taking (W 8)

Convey ideas precisely using appropriate vocabulary (L 3, 6)

Engage in collaborative discussion (SL 1, 2, 4, 6)

Connect:

We have been learning…
…that good readers think about what they know about the genre to help them predict what will happen in the book.

Teach:

Today I am going to teach you...

...that good readers use comprehension strategies to identify important characters and infer character traits. You are each going to make a character list in your reader's notebook as we read chapter 1. The character list will be a tool that we will use while reading this book; it will help us improve our comprehension when we are confused. Today we will also be paying attention to clues about these characters that we find in the story and we will be using these clues to infer character traits.

Watch me as I model how I think about who the important characters are as I'm reading.

Notice how I use clues in the story to help me think about what I know about these characters.

Today we will be using this stem for turn and talk:
When the book said_____, I thought this was an important detail because_____.

Open your reader's notebooks and title a clean page **Character List.** As we create the list together on the easel, you will each copy down the information on a list in your own reader's notebook.

Begin reading chapter 1 of The *Castle in the Attic*, **starting on page 3.**

Model:

Stop after: *"He ran out of the room before she could say anything else."* (p. 4)

So far, we have met two important characters—William and Mrs. Phillips. Let's add these characters to our character list. Now I am going to model how I think about what I know about each of these characters. I'll begin by thinking about William.

When the book said that William was ten years old and old enough to take care of himself, **I thought this was an important detail because** it helps me understand why his housekeeper, Mrs. Phillips, is leaving to go back to England.

I also learned that William is a gymnast.

(Model adding this information to the character list.)

Now I am going to model how I think about the second character, Mrs. Phillips.

When the book said that Mrs. Phillips was homesick and would be going back to England after taking care of William for ten years, **I thought this was an important detail because** it helps me understand why William doesn't want her to go. It also makes me think that Mrs. Phillips is William's nanny.

(Model adding this information to the character list.)

Guided Practice:

Stop after: *"He knew Mrs. Phillips would never leave without them."* (p. 5)

We continue to learn new things about the characters. What else have you learned about Mrs. Phillips?

Turn and talk to your partners using this stem:
When the book said _____, I thought this was an important detail because _____.

(Model adding this thinking and any other important details to the character list.)

Guided Practice:

Stop after: *"I think she'd even leave her picture behind if she had to."* (p. 6)

We met a new character in this section of the text, William's mom. Let's add her to our character chart. We didn't learn much about her in this section of the text, so we will continue to watch for clues about this character as we keep reading.

In this part of the text, we learned new information about William and Mrs. Phillips. What important details did we learn?

Turn and talk to your partners using this stem:
When the book said _____, I thought this was an important detail because _____.

(Model adding this thinking and any other important details to the character list.)

Guided Practice:

Stop after: *"And I'm not going to say one more word about it."* (p. 7)

In this part of the text, we learned new information about William and Mrs. Phillips. What important details did we learn?

Turn and talk to your partners using this stem:
When the book said _____, I thought this was an important detail because _____.

(Model adding this thinking and any other important details to the character list.)

Link:

Today and every day when you read…
…I want you to think about what you know about important characters in order to make a character list for monitoring comprehension.

The following chart is a sample showing what your co-created chart might look like:

Character List

William – 10 yrs. old, gymnast
doesn't want Mrs. Phillips to go
Gentle heart

Mrs. Phillips – housekeeper/nanny
has taken care of William for 10 yrs.
Homesick
will go back home to England
husband was killed in World War II

Mom

Mini-Lesson

Vocabulary Routine: *chivalry* (L 4, 5)

Instructional Read-Aloud

In this chapter…Mrs. Phillips gives William a stone and wooden castle that has been in her family for generations. She tells him that she is entrusting the castle to him because he has "…the kind of gentle soul that accepts the rules of chivalry" (p. 9). Mrs. Phillips introduces William to each room in the castle.

In this lesson…you will be modeling how good readers visualize the setting of the story and use maps to help visualize the setting. Students will be referencing the map of William's castle found at the front of the book. You may want to have this map photocopied so that each student can glue a copy of it into their reader's notebook for reference.

Learning Targets:

Read closely to monitor comprehension (RL 1)
- Infer setting clues
- Visualize

Show understanding of story elements (RL 3)
- Setting

Use what you know about genre to help you understand the story better (RL 5)

Gather and categorize information through note taking (W 8)

Convey ideas precisely using appropriate vocabulary (L 3, 6)

Engage in collaborative discussion (SL 1, 2, 4, 6)

Connect:

We have been learning…
…that good readers determine who the important characters are and think about what they know about the characters based on clues in the text.

Teach:

Today I am going to teach you…

…that good readers pay attention to the setting of the story. Today we will be using the castle diagram from the front of the book to help us visualize one of the settings in our story, William's castle.

Watch me as I model how I think about clues in the story that help me visualize the setting.

Notice how I use the map to help me visualize the setting better.

Today we will be using this stem for turn and talk:
When the book said _____, I thought this was an important detail because _____.

📖 **Begin reading chapter 2 of The *Castle in the Attic*, starting on page 8.**

Model:

📖 **Stop after:** *"The metal grill disappeared into the wall above."* (p. 10)

When the book said that the drawbridge raises and lowers, and that there is a metal grating behind the wooden doors, **I thought this was an important detail because** it tells me that the castle is well protected. I think it probably has to be protected against enemies who might try to attack the castle.

(Model locating the drawbridge and portcullis on the map of William's castle.)

Guided Practice:

📖 **Stop after:** *"…jesters sang to entertain the lords and ladies dining below."* (p. 11)

What else have you learned about the setting of William's castle?

Turn and talk to your partners using this stem:
When the book said _____, I thought this was an important detail because _____.

(Model locating the gatehouse, courtyard, armory, kitchen, and great hall on the map of William's castle.)

Guided Practice:

Stop after: *"I knew you'd like it."* (p. 12)

What else have you learned about the setting of William's castle?

Turn and talk to your partners using this stem:
When the book said _____, I thought this was an important detail because _____.

(Model locating the chapel, rear towers, upper chambers, minstrels' gallery, master's bedchamber, and servant's quarters on the map of William's castle.)

Link:

Today and every day when you read…
…I want you to use clues in the story to visualize the setting.

Instructional Read-Aloud

Topic: King Arthur

In this legend...students will read about King Arthur. The story begins with Arthur as a young child, being raised by a family in the country after his parents' death. The story goes on to tell how he became a page and later a squire under the influence of a young knight, Sir Kay. The legend tells that at age 14, Arthur drew a sword from a stone, making him the rightful king of England. While king, Arthur changed the role of a knight from that of a powerful bully to that of one who honors the Code of Chivalry.

In this lesson...students will gather information about King Arthur. They will read the text like a biography, noting important events and determining what makes this person (King Arthur) so influential.

To prepare for this lesson, make a copy of *The Legend of King Arthur* for each student.

Learning Targets:

Read closely to understand diverse media (RI 1, 2, 3, 7)

Analyze multiple texts (RI 9)

Consider the author's point of view (RI 6)

Gather and categorize information through note taking (W 8)

Convey ideas precisely using appropriate vocabulary (L 3, 6)

Engage in collaborative discussion (SL 1, 2, 4, 6)

Connect:

We have been learning...
...that good readers use outside sources to help them understand the topic of a book better.

Teach:

Today I am going to teach you…

…that good readers stop to learn about real-life people or events when they are important to the text. Yesterday, when we were reading chapter 2, we learned that Mrs. Phillips had been reading William *King Arthur and the Knights of the Round Table.*

Today we are going to read The Legend of King Arthur *in order to understand this historical figure's influence on William.*

As we read, we are going to be thinking about what makes this person, King Arthur, so important. In other words, why is this particular knight more important than others?

As we read, we are going to be highlighting information about him. Please use a highlighter pen or underline in pencil.

Watch me as I model how I look for details about King Arthur that explain why he is so important.

Notice how I highlight this information as I read.

Today we will be using this stem for turn and talk:
When the legend said _____, I thought this was an important detail. This shows that _____ is an important person because _____.

📖 **Begin reading *The Legend of King Arthur,* by Nancy Wolf.**

Model:

📖 **Stop after:** *"There Arthur grew up knowing he was the son of a great man."* (paragraph 3)

When the legend said Arthur was the son of the king of England, **I thought this was an important detail. This shows that** Arthur **is an important person because** he is a prince.

Let's highlight the words in paragraph 2 that say, "…he was the son of a powerful warrior king of England."

The Castle in the Attic Unit of Study

Guided Practice:

Stop after: "They asked Arthur to take it out and he easily lifted the sword from the stone." (paragraph 7)

What did you learn about Arthur here that shows he is an important person?

Turn and talk to your partners using this stem:
When the legend said _____, I thought this was an important detail. This shows that _____ is an important person because _____.

(Model highlighting these important details.)

Guided Practice:

Stop after: "Right requires honor, self-discipline, respect, justice, purity, loyalty, and truth." *(paragraph 10)*

What did you learn about Arthur here that shows he is an important person?

Turn and talk to your partners using this stem:
When the legend said _____, I thought this was an important detail. This shows that _____ is an important person because _____.

(Model highlighting these important details.)

Guided Practice:

Stop after: "This legend encourages people to believe that honor, justice, self-discipline, and truth can create special people, in a special time, in a special place." *(paragraph 16)*

What did you learn about Arthur here that shows he is an important person?

Turn and talk to your partners using this stem:
When the legend said _____, I thought this was an important detail. This shows that _____ is an important person because _____.

(Model highlighting these important details.)

Link:

Today and every day when you read…
…I want you to consider how important people influence the text.

To supplement this lesson, you could check out books relating to the topic from your school library, to be made available to students during independent reading. The following titles are suggestions:

King Arthur:
King Arthur, Jane B. Mason and Sarah Hines Stephens

King Arthur: Tales from the Round Table, Andrew Lang

The Story of King Arthur and His Knights, Howard Pyle, Tania Zamorsky, Dan Andreasen, and Arthur Pober Ed.D.

Knights:
Knight, Christopher Gravett

Knight's Handbook, Sam Taplin

Knights in Shining Armor, Gail Gibbons

Magic Tree House Research Guide: Knights and Castles, Will Osborne and Mary Pope Osborne

The Making of a Knight: How Sir James Earned his Armor, Patrick O'Brien

Outside Text: King Arthur

A legend is a story or stories handed down from earlier times, but may not be totally true. It usually has a hint of the supernatural. Sometimes the hero seems like a superhero.

THE LEGEND OF KING ARTHUR
Nancy Wolf

People who study history have been unable to find out if King Arthur was a real person or not. Stories of him have been around for a long time. People love to think that he really was a person who lived not too long after the Romans left England.

Legend has it that he was the son of a powerful warrior king of England before it organized into a country. When the king was killed in battle, a person named Merlin took the boy to a family in the country to protect him from the king's enemies.

There Arthur grew up not knowing he was the son of a great man. Merlin came one day and took him to a castle where he began learning about how to be a soldier. Arthur took care of the horses, polished the swords, and practiced sword fighting with sticks.

Soon he became a page and learned the ways of the rich landowner. He learned manners, riding tricks, fighting plans and even how to act at dinner. Merlin would come once in a while and teach Arthur things about life and how to get along with people. Some thought Merlin had special magic to help Arthur understand things better.

At fourteen, Arthur was old enough to be a squire for Sir Kay, a young knight from the castle where he was staying. One day Sir Kay and Squire Arthur went to a big tournament. As they were nearing the field where it was being held, Sir Kay realized he forgot his sword.

Arthur ran back to get it. However, along the way, he noticed a sword stuck in a big stone and thought it looked like a better sword. So, he pulled out the sword and took it to Sir Kay. When he showed it to Sir Kay, the people around them realized that it was the sword that had come from the stone.

The tournament was stopped and everyone went to where the stone was. They placed the sword back in the stone and then had several people try to remove it. No one could. They then asked Arthur to take it out and he easily lifted the sword from the stone. The people began cheering, "Long live the king." What Arthur had not seen before was the carving on the side of the stone that said, "Whoever draws this sword from the stone is the rightful high king of England."

Even though Arthur was pretty young, he had learned a lot from many people including Merlin who helped him with making decisions. It was too bad that the country of England was also pretty young and it was hard to get everyone in the country to follow one king. There was lots of fighting among the people of the country.

People finally started to like King Arthur and were willing to fight under his leadership. He viewed the knights as something more than just fighting soldiers. He wanted the people to look up to knights instead of being afraid of them. He wanted the people to know that a knight was there to protect them not to be a bully because he had a bigger sword.

Arthur pushed the idea that being stronger than others does not make it right for you to be mean to them. Having more power does not make it right for you to shove them aside or knock them down. Right requires honor, self-discipline, respect, justice, purity, loyalty and truth.

You may have heard of King Arthur's Round Table at his city of Camelot. The table showed that no one sat in the honored seat at the head of the table because there was no head at a round table. Everyone was of equal importance at Arthur's table.

Some of the most famous knights of legend sat at King Arthur's table. Sir Gawain fought the evil Green Knight. Sir Lancelot was Arthur's favorite knight and Queen Guinevere's champion. Sir Percival went after the people who stole the king's golden goblet. Sir Galahad was considered the best knight at Arthur's table and spent many years looking for the Holy Grail.

Like so often happens, evil tries to battle against good. King Arthur had an evil half-sister who was jealous of him. She spent many years trying to destroy the king, his knights, and his kingdom. She practiced black magic and cast spells on the knights. Sir Mordred, a sly and wicked knight, began planting doubt about Sir Lancelot in King Arthur's mind. Soon, Arthur knew that his wife, Queen Guinevere, loved Lancelot more than she loved him.

When this was discovered, Guinevere was sent to prison. Soon, Sir Lancelot came to rescue her. There was nothing that Arthur could do but go after him and fight against him. The king saw his Round Table knights at war with each other and, before long, many of them were dead. The king, too, was badly wounded.

So, what became of King Arthur? Some say he died of his wounds and was buried on an island. Others say that a mysterious lady came and took him to be with Merlin. It is said that after King Arthur's loss, dark and evil days returned to England where bullies ruled again for a time.

Yet, people still look back on the time of King Arthur, his Round Table and the city of Camelot with hope. This legend encourages people to believe that honor, justice, self-discipline, and truth can create special people, in a special time, in a special place.

Permission to reprint granted by Nancy Wolf, author.

Mini-Lesson

Vocabulary Routine: *tradition* (L 4, 5)
The Latin root 'tra' means *draw together,* and the Latin root 'dit' means *give.* The suffix 'tion' makes this word a noun.

Instructional Read-Aloud

In this chapter…Mrs. Phillips gives William a small box that holds the Silver Knight. She tells the legend about the knight that says one day he will come to life to reclaim his land. In order to follow tradition, Mrs. Phillips suggests that William meet the Silver Knight on his own. At the end of this chapter, William resolves to find a way to get Mrs. Phillips to stay.

In this lesson…you will be modeling how good readers use big clues in the story to predict what will happen. When an author purposely reveals big clues about what might happen, the author is using a technique called foreshadowing. Good readers stop and make predictions when they see an author's use of foreshadowing in the text.

Learning Targets:

Read closely to monitor comprehension (RL 1)
  • Predict

Analyze story elements (RL 3)

Recognize author's craft (RL 4)
  • Foreshadowing

Use what you know about genre to help you understand the story better (RL 5)
  • Predict based on genre

Convey ideas precisely using appropriate vocabulary (L 3, 6)

Engage in collaborative discussion (SL 1, 2, 4, 6)

Connect:

We have been learning…
…that good readers think about story elements as they read.

Teach:

Today I am going to teach you…
…that good readers notice when the author purposely reveals big clues about what is going to happen later in the book. This is called foreshadowing. When good readers see these big clues, they stop and make a prediction.

Watch me as I model how I pay attention to big clues the author purposefully places in the text.

Notice how I use these clues to help me think about what is going to happen next.

Today we are going to use this stem for turn and talk:
When the book said _____, I made a prediction. I was thinking _____.

Begin reading chapter 2 of The *Castle in the Attic,* starting on page 12 where William says, "Are there any knights?"

Model:

Stop after: " *'The castle's really wonderful,' he said again."* (p. 13)

When the book said "You're supposed to meet the Silver Knight on your own," **I made a prediction. I was thinking** that when William meets the Silver Knight, the knight will come alive.

Guided Practice:

Stop after: *"But the whole time I played with the castle, he was stiff and cold as lead."* (p. 15)

Turn and talk to your partners using this stem:
When the book said _____, I made a prediction. I was thinking _____.

Guided Practice:

Stop after: *"He went upstairs to do his homework."* (p. 16)

Turn and talk to your partners using this stem:
When the book said _____, I made a prediction. I was thinking _____.

Link:

Today and every day when you read…
…I want you to stop and make predictions about what will happen next based on big clues the author has given you.

Mini-Lesson

Vocabulary Routine: *friend* **vs.** *foe* (L 4, 5)

Instructional Read-Aloud

In this chapter…the author reveals more information about William's parents. In addition, William opens up the box that holds the Silver Knight. When William touches him, the Silver Knight comes to life.

In this lesson…you will be modeling how readers look for clues about the important characters in the book and then use those clues to infer character traits. Students will be adding these traits to the character list they created in their reader's notebooks on day three.

Learning Targets:

Read closely to monitor comprehension (RL 1)
- Infer character traits
- Visualize

Show understanding of story elements (RL 3)
- Character traits

Use what you know about genre to help you understand the story better (RL 5)

Gather and categorize information through note taking (W 8)

Convey ideas precisely using appropriate vocabulary (L 3, 6)

Engage in collaborative discussion (SL 1, 2, 4, 6)

Connect:

We have been learning…
…that good readers recognize foreshadowing and use the clues that foreshadowing provides to help them predict what will happen in the book.

Teach:

Today I am going to teach you…

…that good readers use comprehension strategies to identify important characters and infer character traits. You are each going to continue to add information to your character list in your reader's notebook. Today we will continue to think about what we know about the characters we already have on our list. We will also be adding new characters to the list.

Watch me as I model how I think about who the important characters are as I'm reading.

Notice how I use clues in the story to help me think about what I know about these characters.

Today we will be using this stem for turn and talk:
When the book said_____, I thought this was an important detail because_____.

Open your reader's notebooks to your copies of our **character list.**

📖 **Begin reading chapter 3 of The *Castle in the Attic*, starting on page 17.**

Model:

📖 **Stop after:** *"The smell of her perfume hung in the air after she'd left."* (p. 18)

In this section of the text, we learned new information about William's mom.

When the book said that William's mom came home after he was already in bed, **I thought this was an important detail because** it helps me understand why William has to have a nanny. William's mom works a lot. She is a pediatrician and is also on the school board. She is a very busy woman.

(Model adding this information to the character list.)

Guided Practice:

Stop after: *"He was being threatened by a seated miniature man waving a pin-sized knife!"* (p. 21)

In this section of the text, William's Dad arrived home from work late. We don't know anything else about him. Let's write his name on the character list, and continue to look for information about him.

(Model adding Dad to the character list.)

We also met the Silver Knight. What did you learn about the Silver Knight?

Turn and talk to your partners using this stem:
When the book said _____, I thought this was an important detail because _____.

(Model adding this information to the character list.)

Guided Practice:

Stop after: *"William fell asleep with his thumb rubbing the small pinprick the dagger had made in his palm."* (p. 25)

What did you learn about the Silver Knight in this section of the text?

Turn and talk to your partners using this stem:
When the book said _____, I thought this was an important detail because _____.

(Model adding this information to the character list.)

Link:

Today and every day when you read…
…I want you to think about what you know about important characters.

Mini-Lesson
Vocabulary Routine: *power* (LS 4, 5)

Instructional Read-Aloud

In this chapter…the author reveals more information about William's parents. Readers also meet Jason, William's best friend. William begins to tell lies to Jason in order to keep the Silver Knight a secret. In this chapter, William becomes even more resolved to keep Mrs. Phillips from leaving.

In this lesson…you will be modeling how good readers infer character traits. As new information is learned about each character, you will be modeling how readers add character traits to a character list.

Learning Targets:

Read closely to monitor comprehension (RL 1)
- Infer character traits

Analyze story elements (RL 3)
- Character

Use what you know about genre to help you understand the story better (RL 5)

Gather and categorize information through note taking (W 8)

Convey ideas precisely using appropriate vocabulary (L 3, 6)

Engage in collaborative discussion (SL 1, 2, 4, 6)

Connect:
We have been learning…
…that good readers identify the important characters while they read and keep a character list.

Teach:

Today I am going to teach you…
…that good readers think about the main character's actions, words, and feelings in order to infer character traits.

Watch me as I model how I look for clues about each character.

Notice how I consider how the actions and words of each character reveal character traits.

Today we will be using this stem for turn and talk:
When the book said _____, I was thinking _____ because _____.

Open up your reader's notebooks to your copies of our character list. We will be adding information to this list today.

📖 **Begin reading chapter 4 of *The Castle in the Attic*, starting on page 26.**

Model:

📖 **Stop after:** *"…William slid a piece of toast and half a slice of bacon into his napkin and tucked them up his shirt sleeve."* (p. 27)

When the book said that William's dad liked architecture and was working on the Harrison's house, **I was thinking** that William's dad is probably an architect **because** architects are involved in designing and building houses.

(Model adding this thinking to the character list.)

Guided Practice:

📖 **Stop after: "Nobody else in their class ever got to school early."** (p. 28)

What can you infer about Jason and William?

Turn and talk to your partners using this stem:
When the book said _____, I was thinking _____ because _____.

(Model adding this thinking to the character list.)

Guided Practice:

Stop after: *"Everything about her made him feel safe and happy."* (p. 30)

What can you infer about Mrs. Phillips?

Turn and talk to your partners using this stem:
When the book said _____, I was thinking _____ because _____.

(Model adding new information to the character list.)

Model:

As we read this next section of the text, we will be focusing on William. His feelings in this part of the text reveal one of the problems in this book. Watch me as I model how I pay attention to Marty's feelings and use those feelings to infer one of the major problems in the story.

Begin reading at the bottom of page 30 where it says, "He grabbed an apple from the bowl..."

Stop after: *"He was so distracted by these thoughts that he almost tripped over the castle."* (p. 31)

When the book said that William knew he had to do something to keep Mrs. Phillips from leaving, **I was thinking** one of the major problems in the book is that Mrs. Phillips is leaving **because** William will do just about anything to get her to stay—including stealing her special things.

Open up your reader's notebooks to a clean page and title it **Problems List.** Let's write down this first problem in the book:
1. Mrs. Phillips is going to leave and William doesn't want her to go.

Link:

Today and every day when you read...
...I want you to think about each character's actions and words and use those clues to infer character traits. Paying attention to the characters is an important strategy that helps readers understand the story better.

The following chart is a sample showing what your co-created chart might look like:

Character List

William – 10 yrs. old, gymnast
   doesn't want Mrs. Phillips to go
   Gentle heart

Mrs. Phillips – housekeeper/nanny
   has taken care of William for 10 yrs.
   Homesick
   Will go back home to England
   husband was killed in World War II

Mom Pediatrician, on the School board
   works a lot, busy

Dad

The Silver Knight – 2 inches,

   Sir Simon

The following chart is a sample showing what your co-created chart might look like:

Problems List

1. Mrs. Phillips is going to leave and William doesn't want her to go.

Instructional Read-Aloud

In this chapter…Sir Simon tells William the story of how he came to be a lead toy.

In this lesson…you will be modeling how readers keep track of important events while reading. You will be focused on keeping track of events in Sir Simon's story.

Learning Targets:

Read closely to monitor comprehension (RL 1)
- Determine importance
- Predict

Show understanding of important story elements (RL 3)
- Plot—important events and problem

Use knowledge of genre to help determine importance (RL 5)
Gather and categorize information through note taking (W 8)
Convey ideas precisely using appropriate vocabulary (L 3, 6)
Engage in collaborative discussion (SL 1, 2, 4, 6)

Connect:

We have been learning…
…that good readers think about the main story elements as they begin reading a book: character, setting, problem, and main events. So far, we have made a character list and visualized the setting of the castle. This work is helping us get the story in our heads so that we understand what we are reading and can think about how the book is going to go.

The Castle in the Attic Unit of Study

Teach:

Today I am going to teach you…

…that good readers think about what events are important, as they read. They also look for the problem and consider how characters plan to solve the problem. Today we will be keeping track of the important events revealed in Sir Simon's story.

Watch me as I model how I look for big events and think about how those events are important.

Notice how I think about the order in which these events happen and why that order is important.

Today we will be using this stem for turn and talk:
When the book said _____, I was thinking this was important because _____.

Open up your reader's notebooks to a clean page and title it **Sir Simon's Story**. Below this title, we will be keeping track of the important events of his story. As we create the chart together on the easel, you will each copy down the information on your own chart in your reader's notebook.

> **Begin reading chapter 4 of *The Castle in the Attic,* starting on page 31, where it says, "Young man, hold up, hold up…"**

Model:

> **Stop after:** *"…they took their time considering the matter of the disease and conferring with one another."* (p. 32)

When the book said that Sir Simon's father, Lord Aquila, became very sick, and the doctors could not cure him, **I was thinking this was important because** it tells about a tragic time in Sir Simon's life.

Let's write our first event under the title **Sir Simon's Story**.
1. Sir Simon's father became very sick, and the doctors could not cure him.

Guided Practice:

> **Stop after:** *"… I sensed even then his desperate need to control people, to have power."* (p. 33)

What were the important events in this part of our text?

Turn and talk to your partners using this stem:
When the book said _____, I was thinking this was important because _____.

(Model adding events to Sir Simon's story.)

Guided Practice:

📖 **Stop after:** *"…after a while he grew secretive around me."* (p. 34)

What were the important events in this part of our text?

Turn and talk to your partners using this stem:
When the book said _____, I was thinking this was important because _____.

(Model adding events to Sir Simon's story.)

Guided Practice:

📖 **Stop after:** *"Alastor was poisoning his mind and his body at the same time."* (p. 35)

What were the important events in this part of our text?

Turn and talk to your partners using this stem:
When the book said _____, I was thinking this was important because _____.

(Model adding events to Sir Simon's story.)

Guided Practice:

📖 **Stop after:** *"Sir Simon stopped speaking and covered his face for a moment."* (p. 36)

What were the important events in this part of our text?

Turn and talk to your partners using this stem:
When the book said _____, I was thinking this was important because _____.

(Model adding events to Sir Simon's story.)

Guided Practice:

📖 **Stop after:** *"I am not small in my own country young man, only in yours."* (p. 38)

What were the important events in this part of our text?

Turn and talk to your partners using this stem:
When the book said _____, I was thinking this was important because _____.

(Model adding events to Sir Simon's story.)

Link:

Today and every day when you read…
…I want you to think about the important events and how those events communicate the problem in the story. This will help you keep the story in your heads.

The following chart is a sample showing what your co-created chart might look like:

Sir Simon's Story

1. Sir Simon's father became very sick and the doctors could not cure him.

2. A wizard named Alastor comes to the castle looking for work and Lord Aquila takes pity on him.

3. Alastor had a magical necklace with
3. tokens. One half of the token made things small and the other half returned them to normal. He used the necklace to shrink rats.

4. Alastor gave Lord Aquila a potion. The potion slowly poisoned him.

5. Lord Aquila died and gave Alastor his kingdom.

6. Calendar & Sir Simon attacked Alastor. Alastor used the necklace to turn Sir Simon to lead.

7. The next thing Sir Simon saw was William.

Mini-Lesson

In this lesson…students will be synthesizing their understanding of Sir Simon's story by writing a summary. Students will be using the retell summary frame to organize their writing. If this is the second time students have practiced using the retell summary frame, they may be ready to write summaries with the support of a partner, or on their own. Students should be expected to produce quality work.

Learning Targets:

Summarize the text (RL 2)
- One sentence sum-up
- Retell summary of the first quadrant

Show understanding of story elements (RL 3)
- Character
- Setting
- Plot

Write an expository piece (W 2)
- Retell events from the beginning, middle, and end of text, in sequence

Write clearly and coherently for task and audience (W 4)

Recall information and draw evidence from the text (W 8, 9)

Write in a short time period (W 10)

Apply and use key vocabulary (L 6)

Convey ideas precisely using appropriate vocabulary (L 3, 6)

Engage in collaborative discussion (SL 1, 2, 4, 6)

Connect:

We have been learning…
…that good readers read slowly at the beginning of the book in order to make sure they understand all the story elements, including character, setting, and plot.

The Castle in the Attic Unit of Study

Teach:

Today I am going to teach you...

...that good readers write a retell summary of the first quadrant of the book in order to monitor their comprehension. When we summarize, we think about the most important events and details from the story. The process of summarizing helps us recognize when we are confused so that we can go back and clear up that confusion.

Today you will be writing a summary of Sir Simon's story, which we read about in chapter 4. You will be using a summary frame to organize the events in his story.

You have already started organizing your thinking about which events are important. Please turn to the page you titled **Sir Simon's Story**. Let's read the events listed there together.

Open up your reader's notebooks and title a clean page **Retell Summary—Sir Simon's Story**. This is a piece of writing that will be graded. Therefore, you will want to do your best work, making sure your writing looks like fourth-grade writing.

You will be using a retell summary frame that will help you organize your thinking about this story. You may also use the important events list to help you with your writing. Remember, you will want to put the events in your own words, adding some details about these events.

Introduce the Retell Summary Frame.

Scaffold:

(Depending on your students' levels of readiness, you will need to decide whether the assignment will be done as:

- Shared writing—written as a group on chart paper or a document camera while students copy this writing into their reader's notebooks.
- Guided writing—started as a group on chart paper or a document camera and then released to be completed collaboratively or independently.
- Collaborative writing—each student works collaboratively with a partner, but is responsible for his or her own writing.
- Independent writing—completed by the student with limited or no guidance.)

Share-out:

(Have students share their writing with their partners or the class. Partners or classmates should respond to students' concluding thoughts from their writing by using the stem:

I agree with you because _____, OR

I disagree with you because _____.)

Retell Summary Frame

Introduction Sentence	*The first quadrant of the book _____, by _____, tells* _____. The introduction should broadly tell what the first quadrant of the book is about.
Body	Describe the most important events from the first quadrant of the book. Include **some** detail. Use transition words such as: *First, next, then, finally,* *First, next, after that, in the end,* *In the beginning, then, after that, finally,*
Conclusion	Describe your thinking about the book. This could be a prediction about what will happen next, an inference about the theme, or a judgment. Use concluding words such as: *In conclusion,* *All in all,* *As you can see,* *It is true,* *I am thinking,* *I predict,*

Adapted from *Step Up to Writing Curriculum* (Auman, 2010)

Retell Summary (Sample):

Sir Simon's story tells about how he became a small, lead toy. First, Sir Simon's father, Lord Aquila became very sick. The doctors could not find a cure for his mysterious disease. Then, one day a wizard named Alastor came to Lord Aquila's castle. Lord Aquila pitied him and gave him a room to stay in. Alastor was secretive and mysterious. Around his neck he wore a magic necklace that had the power to turn objects to lead, make things small, and return them to their normal size. Alastor practiced using the necklace to shrink rats. When Lord Aquila's health became worse, Alastor gave him a potion that seemed to make him better but was actually poisoning him. Finally, Lord Aquila died and gave his kingdom to Alastor. When Sir Simon tried to fight Alastor, Alastor turned Sir Simon to lead and sent him to the toy castle. As you can see, Alastor is a truly evil villain.

I
Interpret the text (1)

- Use comprehension strategies to get to deeper thinking
- Recognize key repeated words and phrases
- Start to think about possible lines of thinking

In this quadrant, readers increase their speed a little bit and reread less. They become more involved in the story.

After finishing this quadrant of the text, readers stop to name a line of thinking and make an evidence collection box.

Days 11–20, Chapters 5–9

Mini-Lesson

Vocabulary Routine: *legend* (L 4, 5)

Instructional Read-Aloud

In this chapter…William has to tell lies and be sneaky in order to keep the Silver Knight a secret. William invites his best friend, Jason, to come to gymnastics practice with him and then to his house so that he can show Jason the castle. William doesn't tell Jason about the Silver Knight. William is tired of lying and blames Mrs. Phillips for the horrible way he feels inside.

In this lesson…you will be modeling how readers think about right and wrong. Students who have already gone through the C. I. A. Unit of Study 4.1 will begin to make connections to *Shiloh,* the read-aloud text in that unit. They will identify that what William is doing—lying and keeping secrets—is wrong.

Learning Targets:

Read closely to monitor comprehension (RL 1)
- Infer

Determine central ideas or themes across texts (RL 2, 4)
- Think about right vs. wrong

Use knowledge of genre to determine importance (RL 5)

Convey ideas precisely using appropriate vocabulary (L 3, 6)

Engage in collaborative discussion (SL 1, 2, 4, 6)

Connect:

We have been learning…
…that good readers pay close attention to the problems in the story and predict how the characters will attempt to resolve those problems.

Teach:

Today I am going to teach you…

…that good readers consider the issues or conflicts within the story and think about how they are important.

Watch me as I model how I think about what the conflicts are.

Notice how I draw conclusions about what the author is trying to say.

Today we will be using this stem for turn and talk:
When the book said _____, I was thinking _____. I think it is right/wrong to _____.

> **Begin reading chapter 4 of *The Castle in the Attic,* starting on page 38 where it says, "The Silver Knight patted the pouch that hung from his belt."**

Model:

> **Stop after:** *"…William added as he went down the stairs."* (p. 40)

When the book said that William came up with a signal for the knight to hide, **I was thinking that** he is keeping a big secret from his best friend and his family. I also am noticing that he has to use lies to cover up his secret. I am thinking keeping a secret is the same as telling a lie. **I think it is wrong to** keep secrets from your friends and family.

Guided Practice:

> **Stop after:** *"It's more fun than practicing the piano."* (p. 42)

Now it is your turn to think about what William is doing and whether or not it is right or wrong.

Turn and talk with your partners using this stem:
When the book said _____, I was thinking _____. I think it is right/wrong to _____.

Guided Practice:

> **Stop after:** *"…he said as he flipped the switch."* (p. 45)

Turn and talk with your partners using this stem:
When the book said _____, I was thinking _____. I think it is right/wrong to _____.

Guided Practice:

> **Stop after:** *"I wouldn't feel this way if she hadn't decided to leave."* (p. 46)

Turn and talk to your partners using this stem:
When the book said _____, I was thinking _____. I think it is right/wrong to _____.

Guided Practice:

Stop after: *"They said no more about the Silver Knight."* (p. 48)

Turn and talk to your partners using this stem:
When the book said _____, I was thinking _____. I think it is right/wrong to _____.

Link:

Today and every day when you read…
…I want you to consider the issues or conflicts within the story and think about how they are important.

Mini-Lesson

Vocabulary Routine: *freedom* vs. *tyranny* (L 4, 5)

The base word 'free' means *enjoying personal rights or liberty.* The suffix 'dom' makes this word a noun.

The Latin root 'tyrann' means *absolute ruler or oppressor,* and the suffix 'y' makes this word an adjective.

Instructional Read-Aloud

In this chapter…William and Sir Simon use the token to shrink a bug. Sir Simon tells William that he is training for battle—he plans on reclaiming his kingdom from Alastor. When William asks how the knight plans on returning to his land, Sir Simon responds by saying, "It will happen when everything is in place" (p. 53). Sir Simon references a riddle that is inscribed above the door of the castle.

William's father makes a visit to the attic and asks William to show him the castle. William's dad decides to make a moat for the castle.

In this lesson…you will be modeling how good readers use important information in the story to predict what will happen. Students will be writing the riddle on page 53 in their reader's notebooks and responding to the riddle with a prediction.

Learning Targets:

Read closely to monitor comprehension (RL 1)
- Predict

Analyze story elements (RL 3)

Use what you know about genre to help you understand the story better (RL 5)
- Predict based on genre

Convey ideas precisely using appropriate vocabulary (L 3, 6)

Engage in collaborative discussion (SL 1, 2, 4, 6)

Connect:

We have been learning…
…that good readers think about right and wrong when they read fantasy books.

Teach:

Today I am going to teach you...
...that good readers notice important information and use that important information to think about what is going to happen later in the book. This is called making predictions.

Watch me as I model how I pay attention to what is important in the text.

Notice how I use this information to help me think about what is going to happen next.

Today we are going to use this stem for turn and talk:
When the book said _____, I made a prediction. I was thinking _____.

📖 **Begin reading chapter 6 of The *Castle in the Attic, starting on page 49.***

Model:

📖 **Stop after:** *"He seemed so sure of himself that William was reluctant to tell him that it was impossible."* (p. 53)

When the book said that the Silver Knight is training to reclaim his kingdom from Alastor, **I made a prediction. I was thinking** that both the Silver Knight and William will go on a quest to defeat Alastor.

Guided Practice:

📖 **Stop after:** *"Until then, I shall prepare myself."* (p. 53)

Do you think this riddle is an important piece of information that might help us make predictions? Please turn to a clean page and copy the riddle into your reader's notebooks.

What are you predicting based on this important information?

Turn and talk to your partners using this stem:
When the book said _____, I made a prediction. I was thinking _____.

Please use the turn and talk stem to help you write your prediction below the riddle.

Guided Practice:

📖 **Stop after:** *"I was just kidding."* (p. 56)

What are you predicting based on this important information?

Turn and talk to your partners using this stem:
When the book said _____, I made a prediction. I was thinking _____.

Stretch it:

Open up your reader's notebooks to a clean page. We are going to copy the riddle written above the entrance to the castle in our notebooks. We know that this riddle is important—it provides a clue as to what might happen in the story.

Below the riddle, please record a prediction that uses evidence from the riddle to support it. Use the stem:

When the book said _____, I made a prediction. I was thinking _____.

Link:

Today and every day when you read...
...I want you to stop and make predictions about what will happen next based on important information the author has given you.

The following chart is a sample showing what your co-created chart might look like:

When the lady doth ply her needle
And the lord his sword doth test,
Then the squire shall cross the
  drawbridge
And the time will be right for a
  quest.

When the book said "who is the lady and who is the squire?" I made a prediction. I think mrs. Phillips is the lady because she is sewing the tapestry. I think William is the squire because he crossed the drawbridge. I also think he will join Sir Simon on the quest to defeat Alastor.

Mini-Lesson

Vocabulary Routine: *unwilling* (L 4, 5)
The base word 'willing' means *cheerfully consenting or ready,* and the prefix 'un' means *not.*

Instructional Read-Aloud

In this chapter… Mrs. Phillips goes with William to his gymnastics practice. It is April, and she will be leaving soon. William has trouble concentrating, knowing that Mrs. Phillips will be leaving. He wishes he could keep her in the palm of his hand. Then he remembers that he can, if he uses the token to shrink Mrs. Phillips.

In this lesson… you be modeling how readers continue to think about the major problem in the book, identifying how the character chooses to solve the problem. Students will be adding the solution to the problems list that they began writing in their reader's notebooks on day eight.

Learning Targets:

Read closely to monitor comprehension (RL 1)

Show understanding of important story elements (RL 3)
* Plot—problem/solution

Gather and categorize information through note taking (W 8)
Convey ideas precisely using appropriate vocabulary (L 3, 6)
Engage in collaborative discussion (SL 1, 2, 4, 6)

Connect:

We have been learning…
…that good readers think about the main story elements as they begin reading a book: character, setting, problem, and main events. When we read chapter 4, we made a problems list in our reader's notebooks.

The Castle in the Attic Unit of Study

Teach:

Today I am going to teach you...
...that good readers continue to think about the problem in the story and consider how a character plans to solve the problem.

Watch me as I model how I look for the problem and think about how the character chooses to solve the problem.

Today we will be using this stem for turn and talk:
When the book said _____, I was thinking this was important because _____.

Open up your reader's notebooks to the problems list we made a few days ago. Today we will be adding the solution to this list.

Begin reading chapter 7 of *The Castle in the Attic*, starting on page 57.

Model:

Stop after: *"But now you're going away, he thought, and that makes everything different."* (p. 59)

When the book said that everything would be different when Mrs. Phillips leaves, **I was thinking this was important because** it tells the problem in the story—that Mrs. Phillips is leaving. William doesn't want things to change. I think he will do anything to get her to stay.

Guided Practice:

Stop after: *"I don't think you'll believe that until I leave."* (p. 61)

Are we learning any more information about the problem in our book?

Turn and talk to your partners using this stem:
When the book said _____, I was thinking this was important because _____.

(Model adding new information to the problems list.)

Guided Practice:

Stop after: *"Of course, he could. With the token."* (p. 62)

What solution did William come up with?

Turn and talk to your partners using this stem:
When the book said _____, I was thinking this was important because _____.

(Model adding the solution to the problems list.)

Link:

Today and every day when you read…
…I want you to think about the problem in the story and how the character chooses to solve the problem.

The following chart is a sample showing what your co-created chart might look like:

Problems List

1. Mrs. Phillips is going to leave and William doesn't want her to go.

   William doesn't believe he can take care of himself.

   ↓

Solution

   William will use the magic token to shrink Mrs. Phillips!

Instructional Read-Aloud

In this chapter…William tells Sir Simon about his idea to shrink Mrs. Phillips. Sir Simon warns William that if Mrs. Phillips comes to the castle unwillingly she will lose time in her own world. On Mrs. Phillips's last day, William's family says goodbye to her. William walks her to the bus stop. When she is not looking, he uses the token to shrink her.

In this lesson…you be modeling how readers think about the similarities and differences between two characters. You will be helping students consider how William's actions make him similar to the evil villain, Alastor.

Learning Targets:

Read closely to monitor comprehension (RL 1)
Show understanding of important story elements (RL 3)
  • Character

Compare and contrast (RL 6)
Gather and categorize information through note taking (W 8)
Convey ideas precisely using appropriate vocabulary (L 3, 6)
Engage in collaborative discussion (SL 1, 2, 4, 6)

Connect:

We have been learning…
…that good readers think about the problem and solution as they read, in order to get the story in their heads.

Teach:

Today I am going to teach you…
…that good readers compare characters when reading, and think about how those characters are similar or different. Today we will be comparing William and Alastor.

What do we know about Alastor?

Watch me as I model how I look for similarities and differences between William and Alastor.

Today we will be using this stem for turn and talk:
When the book said _____, I was thinking _____ and _____ are alike/different because_____.
This makes me think _____.

Open up your reader's notebooks to a clean page. Title the page **William and Alastor**. Then, draw a T-chart below the title. Label the left column **Alike** and the right column **Different**.

> **Begin reading chapter 7 of *The Castle in the Attic* on page 62 where it says, "All that day and the next…"**

Model:

> **Stop after:** *"He would worry about that later."* (p. 63)

When the book said that William put the thought of Mrs. Phillips's feelings out of his mind, **I was thinking** William and Alastor **are alike because** William isn't thinking of Mrs. Phillips's feelings, and Alastor didn't think of other people's feelings either. **This makes me think** that both William and Alastor are selfish.

(Model adding this information to the left column of the T-chart.)

Guided Practice:

> **Stop after:** *"He must not let anything change that."* (p. 64)

Is William showing that he is like Alastor or different from Alastor?

Turn and talk to your partners using this stem:
When the book said _____, I was thinking _____ and _____ are alike/different because_____.
This makes me think _____.

(Model adding this information to the T-chart.)

Guided Practice:

Stop after: "'*Then don't blame me for what happens,*' *he said as he left.*" (p. 66)

Is William showing that he is like Alastor or different from Alastor?

Turn and talk to your partners using this stem:
When the book said _____, I was thinking _____ and _____ are alike/different because_____.
This makes me think _____.

(Model adding this information to the T-chart.)

Guided Practice:

Stop after: *"Now give me a hug and go back into the house."* (p. 68)

Is William showing that he is like Alastor or different from Alastor?

Turn and talk to your partners using this stem:
When the book said _____, I was thinking _____ and _____ are alike/different because_____.
This makes me think _____.

(Model adding this information to the T-chart.)

Guided Practice:

Stop after: *"I want to get you both back up to the attic before anything else happens."* (p. 70)

Is William showing that he is like Alastor or different from Alastor?

Turn and talk to your partners using this stem:
When the book said _____, I was thinking _____ and _____ are alike/different because_____.
This makes me think _____.

(Model adding this information to the T-chart.)

Link:

Today and every day when you read…
…I want you to think about the similarities and differences between characters.

The following chart is a sample showing what your co-created chart might look like:

William & Alastor

Alike	Different
selfish	
want power	
have control over others	
keep secrets	

Mini-Lesson

In this lesson…you will be modeling how readers stop to think about the function of time in fantasy.

Learning Targets:

Read closely to monitor comprehension (RL 1)
- Predict

Show understanding of important story elements (RL 3)
- Setting

Compare and contrast (RL 6)

Connect:

We have been learning…
…that good readers think about how characters are similar and different.

Teach:

Today I am going to teach you…
…that good readers pay attention to the function of time when reading fantasy.

Because fantasy has elements of make-believe, authors can be creative in the use of time in their books. Let's look at how Elizabeth Winthrop uses time in her story, *The Castle in the Attic.*

Begin reading chapter 7 on page 63 where Sir Simon says, "As Alastor once told me…"

Model:

Stop after: *"I will protect her from any harm."* (p. 63)

In this book there are two worlds—the realistic world of William's house, and the fantastical world of Sir Simon's kingdom. The author creates the possibility of people in the real world traveling into the fantastical world. If they do so willingly, it will be as if time doesn't exist. When they decide to return to the real world, they will return to the very moment when they left.

Guided Practice:

Can you think of any other fantasy stories (books, or movies) where time didn't exist in the fantastical world?

Turn and talk.

Guided Practice:

What do you think might happen to Mrs. Phillips in this story?

Turn and talk.

Link:

Today and every day …
…when reading fantasy, I want you to think about the function of time.

Mini-Lesson

In this lesson…students will be drawing a conclusion about William and Alastor. They will consider whether William and Alastor are more alike or more different. The T-chart that they made on day 14 will support them in this work. They will then craft an informal writing piece that organizes evidence proving that William and Alastor are more alike or more different.

Learning Targets:

Analyze story elements (RL 3)
- Character

Draw conclusions about a character's actions; distinguish own point of view (RL 6)

Compare and contrast (RL 9)

Write an expository piece (W 2)
- Comparison writing

Write clearly and coherently according to task (W 4)

Recall information and draw evidence from the text (W 8, 9)

Write within a short time period (W 10)

Apply and use key vocabulary (L 6)

Convey ideas precisely using appropriate vocabulary (L 3, 6)

Engage in collaborative discussion (SL 1, 2, 4, 6)

Connect:

We have been learning…
…that good readers consider how two characters are similar or different. Yesterday we compared William and Alastor. You made a T-chart showing how these characters are alike and different.

Teach:

Today I am going to teach you…

…that good readers draw a conclusion. After comparing two characters, they state whether those characters are more alike or more different. Then, they prove their thinking in writing. Doing this helps readers to think more deeply about a text and to synthesize thinking.

Today you will be writing a comparison paragraph. You will be deciding whether William and Alastor are more alike or more different.

Guided Practice:

Open up your reader's notebooks to the T-chart you made yesterday. Draw a conclusion about William and Alastor—are they more alike or more different?

Turn and talk using this stem:
I think William and Alastor are more alike/different because _____. Also because _____.

Introduce the compare/contrast writing frame.

(Most or all of your students will probably conclude that William and Alastor are more alike than different. Begin by modeling how to write the introduction sentence. For example, "William is a ten-year-old boy from the real world, and Alastor is an evil wizard from the magical world, but for the most part they are very similar.")

Scaffold:

(Depending on your students' levels of readiness, you will need to decide whether the assignment will be done as :
- Shared writing—written as a group on chart paper or a document camera while students copy this writing into their reader's notebooks.
- Guided writing—started as a group on chart paper or a document camera and then released to be completed collaboratively or independently.
- Collaborative writing—each student works collaboratively with a partner, but is responsible for his or her own writing.
- Independent writing—completed by the student with limited or no guidance.)

Share-out:

(Have students share their writing with their partners or the class. Partners or classmates should respond to student writing using the stem:
I agree with you because _____, OR
I disagree with you because _____.)

Compare/Contrast Frame

Introduction Sentence	If the two things are **more alike** than different, begin by saying: _____ is _____ and _____ is _____, but *for the most part they are similar.* If the two things are **more different** than alike, begin by saying: _____ and _____ both _____, *but overall they are very different.*
Body	Explain the ways these two things are either alike or different. Use transition words such as: *First, second, third,* *One way, another way, also,* *First, also, in addition,*
Conclusion	Restate your thinking. Start with one of the following phrases: *In conclusion,* *All in all,* *As you can see,* *It is true,* *To sum up,*

Comparison Writing (Sample):

William is a 10-year-old boy from the real-world, and Alastor is a wizard from the fantastical world, but for the most part they are similar. First, Alastor and William are both selfish because they don't consider other people's feelings. In addition, they both want power and control over others. William wants power and control over Mrs. Phillips and Alastor wants power and control over Lord Aquila's kingdom. Finally, William keeps secrets from his parents, his best friend and Mrs. Phillips. Similarly, Alastor keeps secrets from Lord Aquila and Sir Simon. As you can see, both William and Alastor are behaving like evil villains.

Mini-Lesson

Vocabulary Routine: *disapproval* (L 4, 5)
The Latin root 'prov' means *upright, good, or honest.* **The prefix 'dis' means** *separate or not.*
The prefix 'ap' means *to or toward,* **and the suffix 'al' makes this word a noun.**

Instructional Read-Aloud

In this chapter…William takes the newly shrunken Mrs. Phillips up to the attic. He sees how disappointed she is in him. Mrs. Phillips immediately trusts Sir Simon, and the way the two of them act together makes William feel lonely. Mrs. Phillips refuses to speak with William. Later that night, when William walks past Mrs. Phillips's old room, he realizes that it still feels like she left, even though she is upstairs in the attic. William's father tries very hard to be more involved in William's life and promises to make a moat for William's castle.

In this lesson…you will be modeling how readers infer characters' feelings. You will be focusing on William and Mrs. Phillips in this chapter. Students should pick up on the fact that William's decision to shrink Mrs. Phillips without her consent comes with consequences. At the end of the lesson, students will add this new problem to their problem/solution list.

Learning Targets:

Read closely to monitor comprehension (RL 1)
- Infer character feelings

Show understanding of story elements (RL 3)
- Character
- Problem

Gather and categorize information through note taking (W 8)

Convey ideas precisely using appropriate vocabulary (L 3, 6)

Engage in collaborative discussion (SL 1, 2, 4, 6)

Connect:

We have been learning…
…that good readers recognize how two characters are similar and different, and draw conclusions about those characters.

Teach:

Today I am going to teach you...
...that good readers infer the characters' feelings while reading. Doing this helps readers understand characters better.

Watch me as I model how I look for clues about how the characters in this book are feeling.

Notice how considering the characters' feelings helps me understand the characters better.

Today we will be using this stem for turn and talk:
When the book said _____, I was thinking _____ because _____. This helps me understand _____.

📖 **Begin reading chapter 8 of The *Castle in the Attic, starting on page 71.***

Model:

📖 **Stop after:** *"...he could see she was disappointed by the curve of her shoulders."* (p. 72)

When the book said that Mrs. Phillips didn't move or turn around to look at William, **I was thinking** that Mrs. Phillips is mad and disappointed with William **because** he shrunk her without her consent. **This helps me understand** that William has probably damaged his relationship with Mrs. Phillips.

Guided Practice:

📖 **Stop after:** *"It made him feel oddly lonely."* (p. 73)

What can you infer about William's feelings, and how is that helping you understand him better?

Turn and talk to your partners using this stem:
When the book said _____, I was thinking _____ because _____. This helps me understand _____.

Guided Practice:

📖 **Stop after:** *"It's too dark and creepy up here."* (p. 75)

What can you infer about William's feelings, and how is that helping you understand him better?

Turn and talk to your partners using this stem:
When the book said _____, I was thinking _____ because _____. This helps me understand _____.

Guided Practice:

Stop after: *"Finally he fell asleep with the solid lump of his old bear pushed comfortingly against the lump in his stomach."* (p. 77)

What can you infer about William's feelings, and how is that helping you understand him better?

Turn and talk to your partners using this stem:
When the book said _____, I was thinking _____ because _____. This helps me understand _____.

Model:

We have been keeping track of the problems in the book on our problems list. Please open up your reader's notebooks to that list. Today, we were introduced to a new problem in the book. The problem is that William shrunk Mrs. Phillips against her will, and without the other token, William cannot restore her to her normal size.

(Model adding this new problem to the problems list.)

Link:

Today and every day when you read...
...I want you to think about each character's feelings and how knowing a character's feelings helps you understand him or her better.

The following chart is a sample showing what your co-created chart might look like:

Problems List

1. Mrs. Phillips is going to leave and William doesn't want her to go.

   William doesn't believe he can take care of himself.

   ↓

Solution

   William will use the magic token to shrink Mrs. Phillips!

2. Without the other token, William cannot restore Mrs. Phillips to her normal size.

Mini-Lesson

Vocabulary Routine: *regret* (L 4, 5)
The root 'gret' means *to feel sorry.* The prefix 're' means *after.*

Instructional Read-Aloud

In this chapter... William tries bringing special things for Mrs. Phillips, hoping that she will speak to him. But she remains resolved that she won't speak to William until he restores her to her normal size or until William comes into the castle to get her. Sir Simon asks William to think about becoming small so that William can be the squire in the riddle written above the drawbridge. After having dinner with his father, William decides he will shrink himself.

In this lesson...you will be modeling how readers infer characters' feelings and motivations. Helping students understand how William's love for Mrs. Phillips motivates him to first shrink her and then risk his life for her is an important part of this lesson. Students will add William's new solution to the problem to the problems list in their reader's notebooks.

Learning Targets:

Read closely to monitor comprehension (RL 1)
- Infer character feelings
- Infer character motivations

Show understanding of story elements (RL 3)
- Character
- Problem

Use what you know about genre to help you understand the story better (RL 5)

Gather and categorize information through note taking (W 8)

Convey ideas precisely using appropriate vocabulary (L 3, 6)

Engage in collaborative discussion (SL 1, 2, 4, 6)

Connect:

We have been learning...
...that good readers infer a character's feelings in order to understand the character better.

Teach:

Today I am going to teach you…

…that good readers infer the main character's feelings and think about what motivates him or her to do things. Thinking about the main character's feelings and motivations helps us understand the main character better. Understanding the main character is important when reading fantasy, because the main character will reveal the author's message in the book.

Watch me as I model how I look for clues about the main character's feelings and motivations.

Notice how I consider how these feelings and motivations affect what decisions the main character makes.

Today we will be using this stem for turn and talk:
When the book said _____, I was thinking _____. This helps me understand _____.

Begin reading chapter 9 of The Castle in the Attic, starting on page 78.

Model:

Stop after: *"Every day she spends here she loses time in her own world."* (p. 80)

When the book said that William knew what the knight was thinking—that William had trapped Mrs. Phillips in the castle—**I was thinking** that William realizes that he has done something wrong. **This helps me understand** that it will be up to William to make things right.

Guided Practice:

Stop after: *"'If I'm talking about coming back, I must have decided to go,' he said to the empty room."* (p. 83)

What can you infer about William's feelings, and how is that helping you understand his motivations?

Turn and talk to your partners using this stem:
When the book said _____, I was thinking _____. This helps me understand _____.

Guided Practice:

Stop after: *"They stood there a moment longer without speaking."* (p. 87)

What can you infer about William's feelings, and how is that helping you understand his motivations?

Turn and talk to your partners using this stem:
When the book said _____, I was thinking _____. This helps me understand _____.

Model:

Today in the story, William came up with a new solution to his problem. Let's add this solution to our problems list.

(Model adding the solution to the problems list.)

Link:

Today and every day when you read…
…I want you to think about the main character's feelings and motivations and how they help you understand the main character better.

The following chart is a sample showing what your co-created chart might look like:

Problems List

1. Mrs. Phillips is going to leave and William doesn't want her to go.

   William doesn't believe he can take care of himself.

   ↓

   ## Solution

   William will use the magic token to shrink Mrs. Phillips!

2. Without the other token, William cannot restore Mrs. Phillips to her normal size.

   ↓

   ## Solution

   William will use the token to shrink himself. He will apologize to Mrs. Phillips and then go with Sir Simon to defeat Alastor.

Instructional Read-Aloud

Topic: Becoming a Knight

In this article...students will learn how a young boy is raised from birth to become a knight. Formal training begins at age seven when the young boy is a page; at fourteen he becomes a squire under the internship of a knight; and finally, when the young man proves chivalry he is deemed a knight.

In this lesson...students will gather information about the steps toward knighthood, comparing this sequence of events to William's life. They will use this information to make predictions about what will happen next in the book The Castle in the Attic.

To prepare for this lesson, make a copy of *Becoming a Knight* for each student.

Learning Targets:

Read closely to understand diverse media (RI 1, 2, 3, 7)

Analyze multiple texts (RI 9)

Convey ideas precisely using appropriate vocabulary (L 3, 6)

Engage in collaborative discussion (SL 1, 2, 4, 6)

Connect:

We have been learning...
...that good readers use outside sources to help them understand the topic of a book better.

Teach:

Today I am going to teach you...

...that good readers stop to learn about events when they are important to the text. Yesterday, when we were reading chapter 9, we learned that Sir Simon believes William is the squire the riddle above the drawbridge refers to. In order to understand Sir Simon's thinking, we need to learn about what it means to be a squire. A squire is a young boy, usually around age 14, who is learning to be a knight.

Today we are going to read Becoming a Knight *in order to understand how a young boy becomes a squire and then a knight.*

As we read, we are going to be thinking about whether William has experienced comparable events in his life. We will be considering whether William is indeed a squire.

As we read, we are going to be highlighting information in the text that applies to William. Please use a highlighter pen or underline in pencil.

Watch me as I model how I look for details about becoming a knight that are similar to the life experiences of William.

Notice how I highlight this information as I read.

Today we will be using this stem for turn and talk:
When the article said _____, I thought this was an important detail. This reminds me of _____ because _____.

Begin reading *Becoming a Knight.*

Model:

Stop after: *"The boy would be encouraged to play with toys such as wooden swords and shields in order to mimic the role of a knight." (paragraph 1)*

When the article said that a knight is usually born into a wealthy family, **I thought this was an important detail. This reminds me of** William's situation **because** his family is probably wealthy—his mom is a doctor and his dad is an architect.

Let's highlight the words in paragraph 1 that say, "...born into a noble or wealthy family."

When the article said that the boy was "told stories of brave knights," **I thought this was an important detail. This reminds me of** William because Mrs. Phillips read him stories about King Arthur.

Guided Practice:

Stop after: "A nobleman's wife taught the page manners." (paragraph 2)

Did you notice details that remind you of William?

Turn and talk to your partners using this stem:
When the article said _____, I thought this was an important detail. This reminds me of _____ because _____.

(Model highlighting these important details.)

Guided Practice:

Stop after: "The Code of Chivalry taught bravery, honesty, and loyalty." *(paragraph 3)*

Did you notice details that remind you of William?

Turn and talk to your partners using this stem:
When the article said _____, I thought this was an important detail. This reminds me of _____ because _____.

(Model highlighting these important details.)

Model:

We can also use details in this text to help us make predictions about what is going to happen next in our story *The Castle in the Attic.*

Watch me as I model how I use details in this outside text to help me make predictions about William.

Stop after: "A knighthood ceremony conducted by a knight, noble or king marked the final symbolic step to becoming a knight." *(paragraph 4)*

When the article said that a skilled squire would accompany the knight into battle, **I thought this was an important detail. This reminds me of** William **because** I predict William will go with Sir Simon to battle Alastor.

(Model highlighting these important details.)

Stretch it:

What are you predicting will happen in the story The Castle in the Attic based on details from this outside text?

Turn and talk to your partners using this stem:
When the article said _____, I thought this was an important detail. This reminds me of _____ because _____.

(Model highlighting these important details.)

Link:

Today and every day when you read...
...I want you to consider how important people influence the text.

To supplement this lesson, you might also check out books relating to the topic from your school library, to be made available to students during independent reading. The following titles are suggestions:

King Arthur:
King Arthur, Jane B. Mason and Sarah Hines Stephens

King Arthur: Tales from the Round Table, Andrew Lang

The Story of King Arthur and His Knights, Howard Pyle, Tania Zamorsky, Dan Andreasen, and Arthur Pober Ed.D.

Knights:
Knight, Christopher Gravett

Knight's Handbook, Sam Taplin

Knights in Shining Armor, Gail Gibbons

Magic Tree House Research Guide: Knights and Castles, Will Osborne and Mary Pope Osborne

The Making of a Knight: How Sir James Earned his Armor, Patrick O'Brien

Outside Text: Becoming a Knight

Becoming a Knight
Sarah Collinge

To become a knight, a boy had to go through the steps to knighthood. First, the boy was typically born into a noble or wealthy family, which would have the ability to provide the expensive equipment and weaponry needed to become a knight. From an early age, the boy was taught good manners, and told stories of brave knights. The boy would be encouraged to play with toys such as wooden swords and shields in order to mimic the role of a knight.

Page
Eventually, the boy would become a page on his seventh birthday. As a page, the young boy focused on receiving an education. He was taught religion, riding, swordsmanship, and chess. A nobleman's wife taught the page manners.

Squire
At age fourteen, the page entered the castle and was assigned to a knight. The squire assisted the knight, tending the knight's horse and dressing the knight for battle. The squire continued to ride and learn swordsmanship. The most important duty of the squire was to learn the Code of Chivalry, rules a knight must follow. The Code of Chivalry taught bravery, honesty, and loyalty. As a squire became more skilled, he accompanied the knight into battle. A squire was deemed a knight after proving his honesty, loyalty and bravery. Squires typically became knights around the age of twenty.

Knight
A knighthood ceremony conducted by a knight, noble, or king marked the final symbolic step to becoming a knight.

References:

Knights, squires and pages. Message posted to http://medievaleurope.mrdonn.org

Steps to knighthood. Message posted to http://www.middle-ages.org.uk

Mini-Lesson

Vocabulary Routine: *peace offering* (L 4, 5)
The base word 'peace' means *a state of mutual harmony between people or groups.* The Latin root 'fer' means *to carry or to bring.* The prefix 'of' means *toward or before,* and the suffix 'ing' makes this word a past tense verb.

Instructional Read-Aloud

In this chapter…William realizes that making himself small is risky—he might never return to the real world again. He prepares to enter the fantastical world by packing some items. When his mom tucks him in that night, it is as if he is saying good-bye. The next day, William stands at the draw-bridge, and Sir Simon shrinks him. The chapter ends as William enters the castle.

In this lesson…you will be modeling how readers think about what they know about the genre to make predictions. The genre chart will be a helpful visual during this lesson. Make sure it is easily visible up on the wall.

Learning Targets:

Read closely to monitor comprehension (RL 1)
  • Predict

Analyze story elements (RL 3)

Use what you know about genre to help you understand the story better (RL 5)
  • Predict based on genre

Convey ideas precisely using appropriate vocabulary (L 3, 6)

Engage in collaborative discussion (SL 1, 2, 4, 6)

Connect:

We have been learning…
…that good readers use outside sources to help them understand the story better.

Teach:

Today I am going to teach you…

…that good readers make predictions based on what they know about the genre. Our epic fantasy chart will help us make predictions today.

Watch me as I model how I pay attention to what I know about epic fantasy to help me make a prediction.

Notice how my understanding of the genre helps me think about what is going to happen next.

Today we are going to use this stem for turn and talk:
When the book said _____, I made a prediction. I was thinking _____.

> **Begin reading chapter 9 of** *The Castle in the Attic,* **starting on page 87 where it says, "When William sneaked up later…"**

Model:

> **Stop after:** *"But he knew it was a promise nobody could make to him."* (p. 88)

When the book said William wanted Sir Simon to promise that he would come back to the real world again, **I made a prediction. I was thinking** that in epic fantasy, good overcomes evil. This makes me think that William will return to the real world in the end.

Guided Practice:

> **Stop after:** *"…his bike leaning against his hip, staring after him."* (p. 90)

Turn and talk to your partners using this stem:
When the book said _____, I made a prediction. I was thinking _____.

Guided Practice:

> **Stop after:** *" 'Enter, young William,' was all he said."* (p. 92)

Turn and talk to your partners using this stem:
When the book said _____, I made a prediction. I was thinking _____.

Link:

Today and every day when you read…

…I want you to stop and make predictions about what will happen next based on what you know about the genre.

Mini-Lesson

In this lesson…you will be modeling and guiding students toward ways of thinking about possible themes emerging in this book. At this point, readers should pick one theme to focus on as they read the third quadrant; this is called naming a line of thinking. One way to explain "line of thinking" is to describe it as something the author is trying to teach the reader. In this mini-lesson, students will be reflecting on the first two quadrants of the book in order to consider what the author is trying to teach them. You will help students brainstorm several ideas and then select one to focus on throughout quadrant three.

Learning Targets:

Read closely to monitor comprehension (RL 1)
- Infer theme

Determine central ideas or themes (RL 2)
- Brainstorm possible lines of thinking

Use what you know about genre to help you understand the text (RL 5)
- Theme

Compare stories in the same genre on their approaches to similar themes (RL 9)

Gather and categorize information through note taking (W 8)

Draw evidence from the text (W 9)

Convey ideas precisely using appropriate vocabulary (L 3, 6)

Engage in collaborative discussion (SL 1, 2, 4, 6)

Connect:

We have been learning…
…that good readers use their knowledge of the genre to help them make predictions.

Teach:

Today I am going to teach you…

…that when good readers get to the end of the second quadrant, they stop to consider what themes are emerging in the book. Good readers select a theme to focus on as they read the third quadrant. This is called naming a line of thinking. Today I am going to model how readers consider what the author is teaching them, in order to name several themes. Thinking about what the author is teaching you is considered higher-level thinking

Watch me as I model how I think about what the author talks about over and over again in the book and consider how this pattern might be pointing me toward the theme.

Notice how I think about what I know about the genre to help me think about the theme.

Today we will be using this stem for turn and talk:
I think the author is teaching me _____ because _____.

Model:

I think the author is teaching me that having power over others is wrong, because William realized that shrinking Mrs. Phillips was not the right thing to do.

(Write this idea on chart paper for students to see.)

Guided Practice:

Now it is your turn to think about what the author is teaching you. Since we already have an idea about what the author believes is wrong, now you might want to consider what the author thinks is right. Use the entries in your notebooks to help you.

Turn and talk to your partners using this stem:
I think the author is teaching me _____ because _____.

(Write student responses on chart paper for students to see. If they haven't already done so, nudge students to think about the Code of Chivalry.)

Guided Practice:

Can you think of any other lessons the author might be trying to teach you in this book? Look closely at our genre chart this time to get your ideas.

Turn and talk to your partners using this stem:
I think the author is teaching me _____ because _____.

(Write student responses on chart paper for students to see. If they haven't already done so, nudge students to think about traits of a hero.)

Model:

Let's think about the ideas you came up with. (Read the list of ideas.) When readers select a line of thinking, they pick a lesson that is supported by text evidence. Of the lessons you brainstormed, which ones do we have a lot of evidence for?

Readers also think about picking a line of thinking they are interested in. We have been reading outside texts about knights and becoming a knight. We are really interested in learning about how to follow the Code of Chivalry. We have a lot of evidence to support our idea that following the Code of Chivalry is right. We also know that you must do right to become a knight or a hero.

I think our line of thinking for *The Castle in the Attic* should combine our thoughts about becoming a hero and the Code of Chivalry. Our line of thinking could be that *a hero is someone who follows the Code of Chivalry. As we read, we can be thinking about whether William is proving himself to be the hero in our book.*

Open up your reader's notebooks and title a clean page **Evidence Collection Box**. Below the title please write "**Line of Thinking:** *A hero is someone who follows the Code of Chivalry.*" What are the codes we learned about yesterday? Let's write these (brave, honest, loyal) along the left side of the page. Now draw a large box around what you have written. These boxes are where we will collect all the evidence we have to prove our line of thinking. It will be important to write page numbers next to our pieces of evidence so that we can go back in the text to find our thinking later if we need to.

Model:

When readers name a line of thinking, they go back into the text to see if they have any evidence to support their thinking. First, I am going to recall events from the first part of the book that prove that William is brave.

I think the author is teaching me that a hero is brave and loyal because William was very brave when he shrunk himself and went into the castle. He risked his life for Mrs. Phillips. (Model adding this evidence to the evidence collection box.)

Guided Practice:

Do you recall any other events in the text that prove that William is brave or loyal?

Turn and talk to your partners using this stem:
I think the author is teaching me _____ because _____.

(Model adding this evidence to the evidence collection box.)

Guided Practice:

Do you recall any other events in the text that prove that William is honest?

Turn and talk to your partners using this stem:
I think the author is teaching me _____ because _____.

(Model adding this evidence to the evidence collection box.)

Link:

Today and every day when you read…
…I want you to be thinking about the big idea or theme of the book. Remember that the genre will guide you toward an important line of thinking.

The following chart is a sample showing what your co-created chart might look like:

Evidence Collection Box

Line of thinking: A hero is someone who follows the code of chivalry.

BRAVE: -William shrunk himself to save mrs. Phillips.

Loyal: -William was loyal to mrs. Phillips when he shrunk himself.

Honest: - William cried when he found out mrs. Phillips was leaving.

I

Interpret the text (2)

- Look for evidence to support
  a line of thinking

In this quadrant, readers increase their speed even more and rarely, if ever, reread.

After finishing this quadrant of the text, readers find the turning point and consider how the turning point reveals the author's message. They also predict how the book will end.

Days 21–29, Chapters 10–13

Mini-Lesson

Vocabulary Routine: *mercy* (L 4, 5)

Instructional Read-Aloud

In this chapter…William faces Mrs. Phillips and tells her that he knows he made a mistake. He shares his plan to go with Sir Simon to get the other half of the token. William, Mrs. Phillips, and Sir Simon have dinner together, and William feels happy again and glad he came. William's training with Sir Simon begins. William learns the Code of Chivalry, and swordsmanship. Mrs. Phillips helps William with his gymnastics routine.

In this lesson…you will be modeling how readers look for evidence to support a line of thinking. Model adding evidence to the chart that shows William is beginning to follow the Code of Chivalry.

Learning Targets:

Read closely to monitor comprehension (RL 1)

Determine central ideas or themes of the text (RL 2)

Gather and categorize information through note taking (W 8)

Draw evidence from the text (W 9)

Convey ideas precisely using appropriate vocabulary (L 3, 6)

Engage in collaborative discussion (SL 1, 2, 4, 6)

Connect:

We have been learning…
…that when good readers get to the end of the second quadrant, they stop to think about what the author is teaching them. Readers choose a line of thinking to focus on while reading quadrant three. Yesterday, we chose to focus on the idea that a hero is someone who follows the Code of Chivalry. We already have many strong pieces of evidence to support this line of thinking.

Teach:

Today I am going to teach you…

…that good readers continue to collect evidence to support a line of thinking while reading. This evidence collection will be important in helping us determine the author's message at the end of the third quadrant of the book. Readers can also use the evidence to make a prediction about how the book will end.

Watch me as I model how I think about what events in the text support our line of thinking.

Notice how I think about what I know about the genre.

Today we will be using this stem for turn and talk:
When the book said _____, this supported my line of thinking. William followed the Code of Chivalry when he _____. This proves he is _____.

Begin reading chapter 10 of *The Castle in the Attic*, starting on page 93.

Model:

Stop after: *"The half that sets us free."* (p. 96)

When the book said William knew he had made a mistake by shrinking Mrs. Phillips, **this supported my line of thinking. William followed the Code of Chivalry when he** admitted his mistake. **This proves he is** honest.

(Model adding this evidence to the evidence collection box.)

Guided Practice:

Stop after: *"Tomorrow, my boy, your training begins in earnest."* (p. 97)

What new evidence can we add to support our line of thinking?

Turn and talk to your partners using this stem:
When the book said _____, this supported my line of thinking. William followed the Code of Chivalry when he _____. This proves he is _____.

(Model adding this evidence to the evidence collection box.)

Guided Practice:

Stop after: *"As you wish, my lady."* (p. 98)

What new evidence can we add to support our line of thinking?

Turn and talk to your partners using this stem:
When the book said _____, this supported my line of thinking. William followed the Code of Chivalry when he _____. This proves he is _____.

(Model adding this evidence to the evidence collection box.)

Guided Practice:

Stop after: *"You get back on your feet a little faster that way."* (p. 101)

What new evidence can we add to support our line of thinking?

Turn and talk to your partners using this stem:
When the book said _____, this supported my line of thinking. William followed the Code of Chivalry when he _____. This proves he is _____.

(Model adding this evidence to the evidence collection box.)

Stretch It (Optional):

The evidence we have been collecting in our collection boxes can be used to help us make a prediction about what will happen next.

Turn and talk—share your predictions with your partners. Support your thinking with text evidence.

Link:

Today and every day when you read…
…I want you to be thinking about the big idea or theme of the book. Look for evidence that supports your line of thinking.

The following chart is a sample showing what your co-created chart might look like:

Evidence Collection Box

Line of thinking: A hero
is someone who follows
the code of chivalry.

BRAVE: - William shrunk himself
        to save mrs. Phillips.
-William trains for battle with Alastor.

Loyal: -William was loyal to mrs.
        Phillips when he shrunk
        himself.
-William brought mrs. Phillips a peace offering.

Honest: - William cried when he
        found out mrs. Phillips
        was leaving.
-William admitted he was wrong. p.96

Mini-Lesson

Vocabulary Routine: *knight* (L 4, 5)

Instructional Read-Aloud

In this chapter…Sir Simon declares that he and William are ready to begin their quest. William is anxious about going on his own, but Mrs. Phillips reminds him that this is what she has been trying to tell him all along—that he must learn to find his own way in the world. She tells William that he has "The heart and soul of a knight in the body of a squire" (p. 104). William dresses Sir Simon in his armor, and they both leave the castle.

In this lesson…you will be modeling how readers consider the purpose of multiple plots. The two plots in this epic fantasy are the real-world plot and the fantastical-world plot. The author, Elizabeth Winthrop, has purposefully weaved these two plots together in order to convey her message. You will model thinking about how important it is for William to prove his bravery in the fantastical world in order for him to believe in himself in the real world.

Learning Targets:

Read closely to monitor comprehension (RL 1)
- Infer author's purpose

Determine central ideas or themes of the text (RL 2)

Recognize author's craft (RL 4)
- Multiple plots

Determine the author's purpose (RL 6)

Convey ideas precisely using appropriate vocabulary (L 3, 6)

Engage in collaborative discussion (SL 1, 2, 4, 6)

Connect:

We have been learning…
…that good readers collect evidence to support a line of thinking. We have been thinking about how William is proving that he is a hero and follows the Code of Chivalry.

The Castle in the Attic Unit of Study

Teach:

Today I am going to teach you…

…that good readers notice how the author uses more than one plot to tell the story. They consider why the author purposefully uses more than one plot to tell the story. The two plots in this epic fantasy are the real-world plot and the fantastical-world plot. The author, Elizabeth Winthrop, has purposefully weaved these two plots together in order to convey her message.

Watch me as I model how I think about how the author uses more than one plot to tell the story.

Notice how I think about why the author uses more than one plot to convey her message.

Today we will be using this stem for turn and talk:
When the book said _____, I thought this was important because _____. I think the author wants me to know _____.

📖 **Begin reading chapter 10 of *The Castle in the Attic*, starting on page 102 where it says, "At the end of the week…"**

Model:

📖 **Stop after:** *"In this world and our old one." (p. 103)*

When the book said that William must find his own way in the fantastical world and the real world, **I thought this was important because** Mrs. Phillips is telling William that he has to grow up. **I think the author wants me to know** that growing up is hard because she sends William to fight an evil villain.

Guided Practice:

📖 **Stop after:** *"What would he meet?" (p. 104)*

What is important about these two plots? What do you think the author wants you to know?

Turn and talk to your partners using this stem:
When the book said _____, I thought this was important because _____. I think the author wants me to know _____.

Guided Practice:

📖 **Stop after:** *"When he glanced back the second time, the drawbridge had been raised." (p.107)*

What is important about these two plots? What do you think the author wants you to know?

Turn and talk to your partners using this stem:
When the book said _____, I thought this was important because _____. I think the author wants me to know _____.

Link:

Today and every day when you read…

…I want you to be thinking about the big idea or theme of the book. Look for evidence that supports your line of thinking.

Mini-Lesson

Vocabulary Routine: *tempted* (L 4, 5)
The Latin root 'tempt' means *to influence or to test.* **The suffix 'ed' makes this word a past tense verb.**

Instructional Read-Aloud

In this chapter…William and the Silver Knight travel from the castle to the forest. As they travel, the land becomes wilder. William has the strange feeling that he and Sir Simon are being spied on.

In this lesson…you will be modeling how good readers visualize the setting by creating a setting map. The setting map will be a tool for readers, helping them keep track of important events and predict what will happen next.

Learning Targets:

Read closely to monitor comprehension (RL 1)
- Infer setting clues
- Visualize

Show understanding of story elements (RL 3)
- Setting

Use what you know about genre to help you understand the story better (RL 5)

Gather and categorize information through note taking (W 8)

Convey ideas precisely using appropriate vocabulary (L 3, 6)

Engage in collaborative discussion (SL 1, 2, 4, 6)

Connect:

We have been learning…
…that good readers think about why the author uses more than one plot to convey a message. In this book, the first plot occurs in the real-world setting, and the second plot occurs in the fantastical-world setting.

Teach:

Today I am going to teach you…
…that good readers sketch a map of the setting as they read to help them visualize where and when the story takes place.

Watch me as I model how I look for clues about when and where the story takes place and use those clues to help create a setting map.

Today we will be using this stem for turn and talk:
When the book said _____, I thought this was an important detail because _____. This makes me think _____.

Open your reader's notebooks and title a clean page **Setting Map.** As we create the map together on the easel, you will each copy down the information on your own map in your reader's notebook.

📖 **Begin reading chapter 11 of *The Castle in the Attic*, starting on page 108.**

Model:

📖 **Stop after:** "*'It can be,' was all the knight replied.*" *(p. 109)*

While reading this part of the text, I noticed several important details about where the second plot takes place.

When the book said "The dirt road wound around a corner between two rows of stately trees," **I thought this was an important detail because** it helps me understand that William and the knight are traveling away from the castle. **This makes me think** they have started their quest.

(Model drawing these first setting clues on the map: castle, winding path, trees.)

When the book said they had lunch at a wide, low river with a bridge going across it, **I thought this was an important detail because** it helps me understand what the land around the castle looks like. **This makes me think** that the river is unusually low and I wonder why.

(Model drawing these setting clues on the map: river, bridge.)

This part of the text also gives us information about when the second plot takes place. In the second plot it is summer.

(Model adding the word "summer" to the top of the map.)

Guided Practice:

Stop after: "William had the eerie feeling that the birds were passing word of their progress along to someone ahead." (p. 110)

The author gave us more details about the setting. What were the important details?

Turn and talk to your partners using this stem:
When the book said _____, I thought this was an important detail because _____. This makes me think _____.

(Model drawing these setting clues on the map: thorn bushes, thick trees.)

Guided Practice:

Stop after: *"He was pleased that his voice sounded stronger than he felt." (p. 111)*

The author gave us more details about the setting. What were the important details?

Turn and talk to your partners using this stem:
When the book said _____, I thought this was an important detail because _____. This makes me think _____.

(Model drawing these setting clues on the map: forest.)

Link:

Today and every day when you read...
...I want you to look for clues about the setting.

The following map is a sample showing what your co-created map might look like:

Mini-Lesson

Vocabulary Routine: *apparition* (L 4, 5)
The Latin root 'pari' means *to come into sight*. The prefix 'ap' means *to or toward* and the suffix 'tion' makes this word a noun.

Instructional Read-Aloud

In this chapter…William and Sir Simon travel through the forest. Noises in the forest are almost deafening, and neither of them can see where they are going because of the thickness of the trees. Both are met with temptation. First, William sees a light and is tempted to go toward it off the path. Next, William hears a stream and is tempted to search for it in hopes of a drink. William has to gather strength to resist these temptations. Sir Simon sees his horse, Moonlight, and chases after the apparition, never returning. Finally, William uses his recorder to silence the noise of the birds and animals. Eventually he makes it out of the forest alone.

In this lesson…you will be modeling how readers look for evidence to support a line of thinking. Model adding evidence that shows William is beginning to follow the Code of Chivalry to the chart.

Learning Targets:

Read closely to monitor comprehension (RL 1)

Determine central ideas or themes of the text (RL 2)

Gather and categorize information through note taking (W 8)

Draw evidence from the text (W 9)

Convey ideas precisely using appropriate vocabulary (L 3, 6)

Engage in collaborative discussion (SL 1, 2, 4, 6)

Connect:

We have been learning…
…that when good readers get to the end of the second quadrant, they stop to think about what the author is teaching them. Readers choose a line of thinking to focus on while reading quadrant three. We chose to focus on the idea that a hero is someone who follows the Code of Chivalry. We already have many strong pieces of evidence to support this line of thinking.

Teach:

Today I am going to teach you...

...that good readers continue to collect evidence to support a line of thinking while reading. This evidence collection will be important in helping us determine the author's message at the end of the third quadrant of the book. Readers can also use the evidence to make a prediction about how the book will end.

Watch me as I model how I think about what events in the text support our line of thinking.

Notice how I think about what I know about the genre.

Today we will be using this stem for turn and talk:
When the book said _____, this supported my line of thinking. William followed the Code of Chivalry when he _____. This proves he is _____.

> **Begin reading chapter 11 of *The Castle in the Attic,* starting on page 111 where it says, "They set off again, more slowly this time."**

Model:

> **Stop after:** *"...darkness had closed around them again."* (p. 112)

When the book said William closed his eyes to avoid the temptation of the light, **this supported my line of thinking. William followed the Code of Chivalry when he** didn't believe in something that wasn't true. **This proves he is** honest.

(Model adding this evidence to the evidence collection box.)

Guided Practice:

> **Stop after:** *"...he sank to the ground and cried till he fell asleep."* (p. 113)

What new evidence can we add to support our line of thinking?

Turn and talk to your partners using this stem:
When the book said _____, this supported my line of thinking. William followed the Code of Chivalry when he _____. This proves he is _____.

(Model adding this evidence to the evidence collection box.)

Guided Practice:

Stop after: *"After a few more songs, the road led him out into the middle of a large field."* (p. 116)

What new evidence can we add to support our line of thinking?

Turn and talk to your partners using this stem:
When the book said _____, this supported my line of thinking. William followed the Code of Chivalry when he _____. This proves he is _____.

(Model adding this evidence to the evidence collection box.)

Link:

Today and every day when you read…
…I want you to be thinking about the big idea or theme of the book. Look for evidence that supports your line of thinking.

The following chart is a sample showing what your co-created chart might look like:

Evidence Collection Box

Line of thinking: A hero
   is someone who follows
   the code of chivalry.

BRAVE: -William shrunk himself
          to save mrs. Phillips.
-William trains for battle with Alastor.
-William went through the forest alone.
                                    p. 116

Loyal: -William was loyal to mrs.
          Phillips when he shrunk
          himself.
-William brought mrs. Phillips a peace offering.

Honest: -William cried when he
          found out mrs. Phillips
          was leaving.
-William admitted he was wrong. p. 96
-William didn't believe the apparitions.
                                    p. 112

Mini-Lesson

Vocabulary Routine: *steadfast* (L 4, 5)
The word steadfast is an anglo-saxon compound word. Stead means *place* and fast means *fixed.*
Therefore, steadfast means *fixed in place.*

Instructional Read-Aloud

In this chapter... William meets a young boy, Calendar's grandson. The boy tells William how to get to Alastor's castle and says that "The wizard has left his mark on the land" (p. 117). Since Alastor came into power the crops have died, the animals have gotten sick, the cows won't produce milk, and the wells have dried up.

In this lesson... you will be modeling how good readers visualize the setting and consider cause and effect. You will also be guiding students' thinking about the effects of Alastor's power (evil) on the land.

Learning Targets:

Read closely to monitor comprehension (RL 1)
- Infer setting clues
- Visualize

Show understanding of story elements (RL 3)
- Setting

Use what you know about genre to help you understand the story better (RL 5)

Convey ideas precisely using appropriate vocabulary (L 3, 6)

Engage in collaborative discussion (SL 1, 2, 4, 6)

Connect:

We have been learning...
...that good readers sketch a map of the setting as they read to help them visualize where and when the story takes place.

Teach:

Today I am going to teach you…

…that good readers use the setting map to think about cause and effect. In this chapter, we will learn that Alastor's evil power has had an effect on the land.

Watch me as I model how I look for clues about how Alastor's power has changed the land.

Today we will be using this stem for turn and talk:
When the book said _____, I thought this was a consequence of _____. This makes me think _____.

Begin reading chapters 11 and 12 of *The Castle in the Attic*, starting on page 116 where it says, "William slipped his recorder into his pouch…"

Model:

Stop after: *"They say everybody is Alastor's spy." (p. 118)*

While reading this part of the text, I noticed several important details about where the second plot takes place. These details are making me think about Alastor's effect on the land.

When the book said the crops have died, the animals have gotten sick, the cows won't produce milk, and the wells have dried up, **I thought this was a consequence of Alastor's evil ways. This makes me think** that when people do things that are bad, there will be consequences.

Guided Practice:

Stop after: "Although it was full summer, only a few ears of corn and some stunted grain grew in the dry brown fields." (p. 120)

The author gave us more details about the setting. What are these details making you think about Alastor's effect on the land?

Turn and talk to your partners using this stem:
When the book said _____, I thought this was a consequence of _____. This makes me think _____.

Guided Practice:

Stop after: "*The water tasted brackish, and he took only enough to wet his mouth.*" (p. 121)

Brackish means unpleasant, salty.

The author gave us more details about the setting. What are these details making you think about Alastor's effect on the land?

Turn and talk to your partners using this stem:
When the book said _____, I thought this was a consequence of _____. This makes me think _____.

Link:

Today and every day when you read…
…I want you to look for clues about the setting and think about what these clues tell you about cause and effect.

Mini-Lesson

Vocabulary Routine: *compassionate* (L 4, 5)
The Latin root 'pari' means *to come into sight*. The prefix 'ap' means *to or toward* and the suffix 'tion' makes this word a noun.

Instructional Read-Aloud

In this chapter... William shows compassion to an old man who is hungry. He climbs a very tall tree to retrieve an apple for the old man. Despite the temptation to look down and to eat the apple himself, William follows the man's instructions. When he gives the apple to the old man, the old man takes a bite and is transformed into a much younger man. The man tells William that William has broken the spell put on him by the evil Wizard.

In this lesson...you will be modeling how readers look for evidence to support a line of thinking. Model adding evidence that shows William is beginning to follow the Code of Chivalry to the chart.

Learning Targets:

Read closely to monitor comprehension (RL 1)

Determine central ideas or themes of the text (RL 2)

Gather and categorize information through note taking (W 8)

Draw evidence from the text (W 9)

Convey ideas precisely using appropriate vocabulary (L 3, 6)

Engage in collaborative discussion (SL 1, 2, 4, 6)

Connect:

We have been learning...
...that good readers keep track of important story elements when a second plot is revealed.

Teach:

Today I am going to teach you...

...that good readers continue to collect evidence to support a line of thinking while reading. This evidence collection will be important in helping us determine the author's message at the end of the third quadrant of the book. Readers can also use the evidence to make a prediction about how the book will end.

Watch me as I model how I think about what events in the text support our line of thinking.

Notice how I think about what I know about the genre.

Today we will be using this stem for turn and talk:
When the book said _____, this supported my line of thinking. William followed the Code of Chivalry when he _____. This proves he is _____.

Begin reading chapter 12 of *The Castle in the Attic*, starting on page 121 where it says, "He knew by the position of the sun..."

Model:

Stop after: *"How can I help you, sir?"* (p. 122)

When the book said William remembered that the Code of Chivalry says to be compassionate to the needy, **this supported my line of thinking. William followed the Code of Chivalry when he** asked the old man, "how can I help you, sir?" even though he was in a hurry. **This proves he is** compassionate.

(Model adding this evidence to the evidence collection box.)

Guided Practice:

Stop after: *"Don't stray off the path."* (p. 124)

What new evidence can we add to support our line of thinking?

Turn and talk to your partners using this stem:
When the book said _____, this supported my line of thinking. William followed the Code of Chivalry when he _____. This proves he is _____.

(Model adding this evidence to the evidence collection box.)

Guided Practice:

Stop after: *"I have been imprisoned inside that old man's shape for years."* (p. 126)

What new evidence can we add to support our line of thinking?

Turn and talk to your partners using this stem:
When the book said _____, this supported my line of thinking. William followed the Code of Chivalry when he _____. This proves he is _____.

(Model adding this evidence to the evidence collection box.)

Guided Practice:

Stop after: *"Perhaps that will get me into the castle."* (p. 128)

What new evidence can we add to support our line of thinking?

Turn and talk to your partners using this stem:
When the book said _____, this supported my line of thinking. William followed the Code of Chivalry when he _____. This proves he is _____.

(Model adding this evidence to the evidence collection box.)

Model:

We learned some new information about the setting in this section of the text. Please open up your reader's notebooks to the setting map.

What important details about the setting can we add to our map?

(Model adding new setting information to the setting map.)

Link:

Today and every day when you read…
…I want you to be thinking about the big idea or theme of the book. Look for evidence that supports your line of thinking.

The following chart is a sample showing what your co-created chart might look like:

Evidence Collection Box

Line of thinking: A hero
is someone who follows
the code of chivalry.

BRAVE: - William shrunk himself
to save Mrs. Phillips.
- William trains for battle with Alastor.
- William went through the forest alone.
p.116
- William decides to go to the castle
to become Alastor's fool. p.128

Loyal: - William was loyal to Mrs.
Phillips when he shrunk
himself.
- William brought Mrs. Phillips a peace offering.

Honest: - William cried when he
found out Mrs. Phillips
was leaving.
- William admitted he was wrong. p.96
- William didn't believe the apparitions.
p.112

More evidence

Compassionate:

- William asked the old man, "How can I help you?" p.122
- William climbs a tall tree to get the old man an apple p.124
- William broke the curse p.126

The following map is a sample showing what your co-created map might look like:

Mini-Lesson

Vocabulary Routine: *foolish* vs. *wise* (L 4, 5)
The base word 'fool' means *someone who is lacking judgment, sense, or understanding.*
The suffix 'ish' means *characteristic of or like* and makes this word an adjective. The word 'wise'
means *having or showing knowledge, understanding, or good judgment.*

Instructional Read-Aloud

In this chapter…William tells the young man, Dick, about his plans to go to the wizard's castle.
Dick tells William that he is the son-in-law of Calendar. At one time, Calendar told the young man
how to defeat the dragon, who is really Calendar's cat, transformed. The young man passes this secret on to William. As they part ways, Dick recalls a legend about a boy who would come back to
save the kingdom.

In this lesson…you will be modeling how readers keep track of important characters in this new
plot while reading. Because the characters are all part of a family, you will use a family tree to organize the character list.

Learning Targets:

Read closely to monitor comprehension (RL 1)
  • Infer character traits
  • Visualize

Show understanding of story elements (RL 3)
  • Character traits

Use what you know about genre to help you understand the story better (RL 5)

Gather and categorize information through note taking (W 8)

Convey ideas precisely using appropriate vocabulary (L 3, 6)

Engage in collaborative discussion (SL 1, 2, 4, 6)

Connect:

We have been learning…
…that good readers collect evidence to support a line of thinking.

The Castle in the Attic Unit of Study

Teach:

Today I am going to teach you…

…that good readers keep track of important characters in the second plot in order to monitor their comprehension while reading.

Watch me as I model how I think about who the important characters are as I'm reading.

Notice how I use clues in the story to help me think about what I know about these characters.

Today we will be using this stem for turn and talk:
When the book said_____, I thought this was an important detail because_____.

Open your reader's notebooks and title a clean page **Character list.** Today we will be organizing our information into a family tree, since many of the characters introduced in the fantastical plot are related. As we create the list together on the easel, you will each copy down the information on a list in your own reader's notebook. Make sure you copy the information exactly as I have it written on the chart in order to show the relationship of the characters to each other.

📖 **Begin reading chapter 12 of *Castle in the Attic*, starting on page 128 where it says, "In some ways, you are quite the fool, my boy."**

Model:

📖 **Stop after:** *"But I will tell you what I know." (p. 128)*

We know that in this fantastical world, Sir Simon represents good and Alastor represents evil. They are the leaders of this land. Please write these two names beside each other at the top of your character list.

When the book said Dick's "wife's mother was Calendar, the nurse to Simon, the King's son," **I thought this was an important detail because** it helps me understand how Calendar is related to all the characters in this second plot. I am going to put Calendar at the top of my family tree.

(Model adding Calendar, Calendar's daughter, and Dick to the family tree. Also include information about these characters. Use the sample character list as a guide.)

Guided Practice:

Stop after: *"He told me that his grandmother was the Silver Knight's nurse."* (p. 129)

What other character can we add to our family tree?

Turn and talk to your partners using this stem:
When the book said _____, I thought this was an important detail because _____.

(Model adding Tolliver to the family tree.)

Guided Practice:

Stop after: *"And he stood there waving until William turned the corner."* (p. 130)

How is William important in this second plot?

Turn and talk to your partners using this stem:
When the book said _____, I thought this was an important detail because _____.

Link:

Today and every day when you read...
...I want you to think about what you know about important characters in order to make a character list for monitoring comprehension.

The following chart is a sample showing what your co-created chart might look like:

Character List

Sir Simon   Alastor

Calendar
- Sir Simon's nurse
- Lives with Alastor

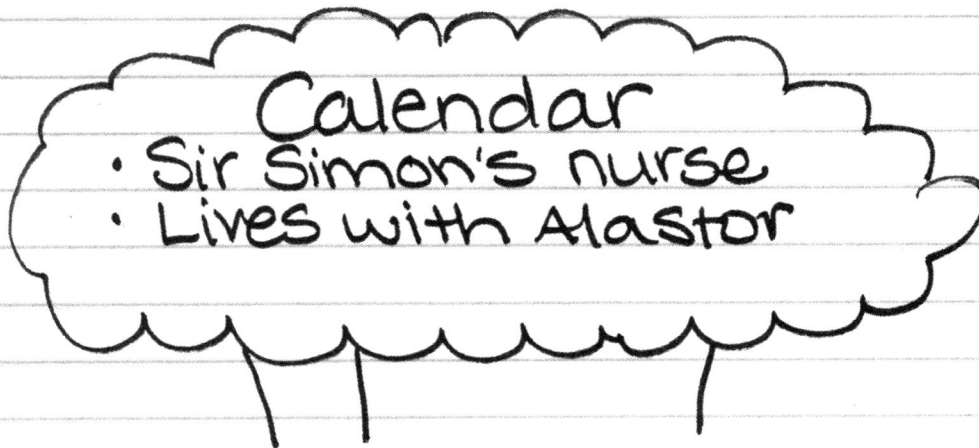

Daughter — Dick (cursed by Alastor)

Tolliver
(the boy William met outside the forest)

Mini-Lesson

Vocabulary Routine: *courage* L 4, 5)
The Latin root 'cour' means *heart*. The suffix 'age' makes this word a noun.

Instructional Read-Aloud

In this chapter... William is traveling to the castle. He hears people passing by talking about the man and boy who were turned to lead. William knows they are talking about Sir Simon and Tolliver, but he tries not to think about it. William feels very alone. He almost gives up, but finally resolves to go to the castle. He uses his recorder to calm the dragon, but is almost overcome by the terrible scenes in the eyes of the dragon. Finally, William stabs the dragon with his dagger. The dragon is now under William's control. The chapter ends as William knocks on the castle door.

In this lesson...you will begin by telling students that today they will reach the turning point of the book, and you'll explain that the turning point is where the plot makes a dramatic change and where the author reveals her message. Students will use their evidence collection boxes to consider what the turning point might be. You will model for students how thinking about what is most important helps you to predict the turning point. A final piece of evidence will be added to the evidence collection box: "William knocks on the castle door." Help students understand that only a true hero—one who follows the Code of Chivalry—would be able to overcome all the tests and safely knock on the door of the castle. William is the boy from the legend.

Learning Targets:

Read closely to monitor comprehension (RL 1)
- Determine Importance
- Predict

Determine central ideas or themes (RL 2)

Analyze story elements (RL 3)
- Plot—turning point

Use what you know about structure and genre to help you understand the story better (RL 5)
- Turning point

Describe how the turning point reveals the author's message (RL 2, 4, 6)

Gather and categorize information through note taking (W 8)

Draw evidence from the text (W 9)

Convey ideas precisely using appropriate vocabulary (L 3, 6)

Engage in collaborative discussion (SL 1, 2, 4, 6)

Connect:

We have been learning…
…that good readers keep track of important characters when a new plot is introduced.

We have also been learning that readers use a variety of strategies to understand what they are reading. Readers use different strategies depending on where they are in the book.

Teach:

Today I am going to teach you…

…that good readers, as they approach the end of the third quadrant of the book, look for the turning point in the story. At the turning point, the plot changes dramatically. The turning point is the most important event in the whole book because it will change the way the story is going to go. It will also reveal the author's message.

Our line of thinking in this book is that William will follow the Code of Chivalry and prove himself to be the hero.

Watch me as I model how I look for clues that the story is going to change dramatically.

Notice how I also predict how the plot will change.

Today we will be using this stem for turn and talk:
When the book said _____, I was thinking this was an important event because _____. This makes me think _____.

📖 **Begin reading chapter 13 of *The Castle in the Attic, starting on page 131.***

Model:

📖 **Stop after:** *"So he took the thought right out of his mind and left it sitting there on the side of the road." (p. 132)*

When the book said that the Silver Knight had been turned to lead, **I was thinking this was an important event because** it shows that William will have to fight Alastor on his own. **This makes me think** that William will be the hero of the story.

Guided Practice:

📖 **Stop after:** *"Once he started walking toward the dragon, there would be no turning back."* (p. 133)

Turn and talk to your partners using this stem:
When the book said _____, I was thinking this was an important event because _____. This makes me think _____.

Guided Practice:

📖 **Stop after: "William sank to his knees in the dirt and let the recorder drop from his mouth."** (p. 137)

Turn and talk to your partners using this stem:
When the book said _____, I was thinking this was an important event because _____. This makes me think _____.

Guided Practice:

📖 **Stop after:** *"Then he marched across the drawbridge right up to the door and knocked loudly three times."* (p. 139)

Turn and talk to your partners using this stem:
When the book said _____, I was thinking this was an important event because _____. This makes me think _____.

Model:

We know that the turning point is the point at which the plot makes a dramatic change. We also know that the turning point will reveal the author's message.

What is the turning point in our book?

(Model adding the words "William knocks on the door" to the evidence collection box. Circle this piece of evidence to note that these words mark the turning point.)

Link:

Today and every day when you read...
...I want you to watch for the turning point near the end of the third quadrant of the book and predict how the turning point might change the plot dramatically.

The following chart is a sample showing what your co-created chart might look like:

Evidence Collection Box

Line of thinking: A hero
is someone who follows
the code of chivalry.

BRAVE: -William shrunk himself
to save mrs. Phillips.
-William trains for battle with Alastor.
-William went through the forest alone.
P. 116

-William decides to go to the castle
to become Alastor's fool. P. 128
-William defeats the dragon & knocks
on the castle door.   P. 139   ★ ←   Turning Point!

Loyal: -William was loyal to mrs.
Phillips when he shrunk
himself.
-William brought mrs. Phillips a peace offering.

Honest: -William cried when he
found out mrs. Phillips
was leaving.
-William admitted he was wrong. p. 96
-William didn't believe the apparitions.
p. 112

Mini-Lesson

In this lesson…students will be naming the turning point and considering how this event changes the plot. In addition, they will be using the turning point as evidence of the author's message. Students will be using the turning point frame to organize their writing. If this is the first time that your students have used this frame, I recommend completing the assignment as shared writing. If students have used the frame in the previous unit, release them to complete the writing with a partner or independently. Students may use their evidence collection boxes to help them with their writing. Students should be expected to produce quality work.

Learning Targets:

Determine central ideas or themes (RL 2)

Use what you know about structure and genre to help you understand the story better (RL 5)
- Turning point

Describe how the turning point reveals the author's message (RL 2, 6)
- Author's perspective
- Own perspective

Write an expository piece (W 1)

Write clearly and coherently for task and audience (W 4)

Recall information and draw evidence from the text (W 8, 9)

Write in a short time period (W 10)

Apply and use key vocabulary (L 6)

Convey ideas precisely using appropriate vocabulary (L 3, 6)

Engage in collaborative discussion (SL 1, 2, 4, 6)

Connect:

We have been learning…
…that as they approach the end of the third quadrant of the book, good readers look for the turning point. The turning point is the place in the text where the plot makes a dramatic change. Yesterday we determined that the turning point in *The Castle in the Attic* is when William knocks on the door of the castle, alone.

Teach:

Today I am going to teach you…

…that good readers write a short response when they reach the turning point in order to monitor their comprehension and get to deeper thinking about the book.

You will be using a template in your reader's notebooks to organize your thinking about the turning point.

Open up your reader's notebooks and title a clean page **Turning Point Writing**. This is a piece of writing that will be graded. You will want to do your best work, making sure your writing looks like fourth-grade writing.

Introduce the Turning Point Frame.

Scaffold:

(Depending on your students' levels of readiness, you will need to decide whether the assignment will be done as :
- Shared writing—written as a group on chart paper or a document camera while students copy this writing into their reader's notebooks.
- Guided writing—started as a group on chart paper or a document camera and then released to be completed collaboratively or independently.
- Collaborative writing—each student works collaboratively with a partner, but is responsible for his or her own writing.
- Independent writing—completed by the student with limited or no guidance.)

Share-out:

(Have students share their writing with their partners or the class. Partners or classmates should respond to students' concluding thoughts from their writing by using the stem:
I agree with you because _____, OR
I disagree with you because _____.)

Turning Point Frame

I think the turning point of the book is…

This will change the plot because…

I think this event tells me that the author's message is…

because…

Turning Point Writing (Sample):

I think the turning point of the book is when William defeats the dragon by himself and knocks on Alastor's door. This will change the plot because now William is brave and he believes in himself. I think this event tells me that the author's message is anyone can be a hero as long as they are brave and believe in themselves. I think this because at first William didn't think he could do anything without Mrs. Phillips or the Silver Knight, but now he made it through the forest alone and defeated the dragon alone.

A
Apply to Your Life

- Continue to look for evidence to support a line of thinking
- Confirm/revise predictions
- Think about problems/solutions/results
- Evaluate how the author ties up the loose ends
- Evaluate the author's message
- Consider how the book will impact your life

In this quadrant, readers read without interruption to the end.

After finishing this quadrant of the text, readers reflect on their reading by summarizing, synthesizing, and evaluating.

Days 30–38, Chapters 14–17

Mini-Lesson

Vocabulary Routine: *imprisoned* **vs.** *freed* **(L 4, 5)**
The base word 'prison' means *a place or situation from which you cannot escape.* The prefix
'im' means *in, into, or inside.* The suffix 'ed' makes this word a past tense verb. The word 'free'
means *not physically held by something.* The suffix 'ed' makes this word a past tense verb.

Instructional Read-Aloud

In this chapter…William meets Alastor. He introduces himself as Muggins and tells Alastor that
he hopes to be Alastor's fool. Alastor agrees to let William stay at the castle and be his jester. Alastor takes William to the room where he keeps all the people he has turned to lead. William sees Sir
Simon and Tolliver.

In this lesson…you will be modeling how good readers use the turning point and the author's message to make a prediction about how the story will end.

Learning Targets:

Read closely to monitor comprehension (RL 1)
  • Predict

Use what you know about genre to help you understand the story better (RL 5)
  • Predict based on genre

Consider the author's perspective (RL 6)

Convey ideas precisely using appropriate vocabulary (L 3, 6)

Engage in collaborative discussion (SL 1, 2, 4, 6)

Connect:

We have been learning…
…that good readers look for the turning point and determine how it reveals the author's message.

Teach:

Today I am going to teach you…

…that good readers make predictions about how the book will end based on the turning point.

Watch me as I model how I pay attention to the clues in the text that will help me make a prediction.

Notice how I use these clues to help me think about what is going to happen next.

Today we will be using this stem for turn and talk:
When the book said _____, I made a prediction. I was thinking _____.

Begin reading chapter 14 of *The Castle in the Attic*, starting on page 140.

Model:

Stop after: *"'No sir,' William ventured warily."* (p. 144)

When the book said that Alastor took William's dagger, **I made a prediction. I was thinking** that in the end, William will have to use other weapons to defeat Alastor. Maybe he will use his gymnastics tricks.

Guided Practice:

Stop after: *"How was he ever going to do that?"* (p. 146)

Turn and talk to your partners using this stem:
When the book said _____, I made a prediction. I was thinking _____.

Guided Practice:

Stop after: *"…using it for a pillow, he went to sleep."* (p. 148)

Turn and talk to your partners using this stem:
When the book said _____, I made a prediction. I was thinking _____.

Link:

Today and every day when you read…

…I want you to stop and make predictions about what will happen next based on evidence the author has given you.

Instructional Read-Aloud (Read-in)

In this lesson…you will be modeling how readers read without interruption as they near the end of the book. Rather than stopping to model a specific strategy or skill, you will simply read. Stop to allow turn and talk only when students will be eager to share their thinking with their partners. Keep the turn and talk stem general so that students can share any type of thinking about the text. This lesson requires an uninterrupted block of time during which you can read all the way to the end of the book. It is important that our students get to experience the same enjoyable feeling of reading to the end that lifelong readers find so satisfying.

Learning Targets:

Read closely to monitor comprehension (RL 1)

Determine central ideas or themes of the text (RL 2)

Consider the author's perspective (RL 6)

Convey ideas precisely using appropriate vocabulary (L 3, 6)

Engage in collaborative discussion (SL 1, 2, 4, 6)

Connect:

We have been learning…
…that good readers use a variety of strategies to understand what they are reading. Readers use different strategies depending on where they are in the book.

Teach:

Today I am going to teach you…
…that good readers, once they reach the turning point, read without interruption to the end, in order to enjoy the satisfying feeling of finishing a book. As they get ready to do that, they think about how the author is going to "tie up all the loose ends" at the end.

Today we are going to use this stem for turn and talk:
When the book said _____, I was thinking _____ because _____.

📖 **Begin reading chapters 15–17 of *The Castle in the Attic,* starting on page 149.**

(Stop for turn and talk only when it is important for students' processing of the text. Use this open-ended stem:
When the book said _____, I was thinking _____ because _____.)

Link:

Today and every day when you read...

...I want you to stop after finishing a book and evaluate the author's work.

- Do you like how the author ended the book?
- Did the author answer all your questions?
- Do you agree with the author's message?
- Would you consider reading the sequel to *The Castle in the Attic (The Battle for the Castle)?*

(Allow time for students to evaluate the author's work in discussion, either with their turn and talk partners or as a whole group.)

Mini-Lesson

In this lesson...students will synthesize the entire text. Summarizing is more rigorous here than at the end of quadrant one, as students are being asked to synthesize a much larger portion of text. Students will use a frame very similar to the retell summary frame. This frame requires students to retell only the most important events and limit the amount of detail used to describe these events. When summarizing the entire book, it is important to include the most important event—the turning point. Students should be expected to produce quality work.

Learning Targets:

Determine theme and summarize text (RL 2)
- Synthesis summary

Write an expository piece (W 2)
- Synthesis summary

Write clearly and coherently for task and audience (W 4)

Recall information and draw evidence from the text (W 8, 9)

Write in a short time period (W 10)

Apply and use key vocabulary (L 6)

Convey ideas precisely using appropriate vocabulary (L 3, 6)

Engage in collaborative discussion (SL 1, 2, 4, 6)

Connect:

We have been learning...
...that good readers write in order to monitor their comprehension while reading and get to deeper thinking.

Teach:

Today I am going to teach you…

…that good readers write a summary after reading in order to synthesize what they have read. When you synthesize information, you combine all of your thinking to help you understand the book better.

Today you will be using the synthesis summary frame to write a summary of the whole book. Be very careful to include only the most important events; the summary should be no more than eight sentences long.

You have each already written a retell summary of the first quadrant of the book. You have also collected a great deal of information in your reader's notebooks. Today you will be using that previous work to help you with your synthesis summaries.

Open up your reader's notebooks and title a clean page **Synthesis Summary**. This is a piece of writing that will be graded. You will want to do your best work, making sure your writing looks like fourth-grade writing.

You will be using a synthesis summary frame that will help you organize your thinking about this book. You may also use the charts in your notebook to help you with your writing.

Introduce the Synthesis Summary Frame.

Scaffold:

(Depending on your students' levels of readiness, you will need to decide whether the assignment will be done as :
- Shared writing—written as a group on chart paper or a document camera while students copy this writing into their reader's notebooks.
- Guided writing—started as a group on chart paper or a document camera and then released to be completed collaboratively or independently.
- Collaborative writing—each student works collaboratively with a partner, but is responsible for his or her own writing.
- Independent writing—completed by the student with limited or no guidance.)

Share-out:

(Have students share their writing with their partners or the class. Partners or classmates should respond to students' concluding thoughts from their writing by using the stem:

I agree with you because _____, OR

I disagree with you because _____.)

Synthesis Summary Frame

Introduction Sentence	The book _____, by _____ tells _____. This paragraph should broadly tell what the whole book is about and include the theme or author's message.
Body	Tell all of the **most** important events from the book. Include **limited** detail. Make sure the turning point is included in your summary. Use transition words such as: *First, next, then, finally,* *First, next, after that, in the end,* *In the beginning, then, after that, finally,*
Conclusion	Your conclusion will reveal the author's message. Use concluding words such as: *In conclusion,* *All in all,* *As you can see,* *It is true,* *I am thinking,* *I predict,*

Adapted from *Step Up to Writing Curriculum* (Auman, 2010)

Synthesis Summary (Sample):

The Castle in the Attic by Elizabeth Winthrop tells the story of a boy who becomes a hero by following the Code of Chivalry. First, William is told that his nanny, Mrs. Phillips is leaving after taking care of him for 10 years. William is determined to make her stay. Mrs. Phillips gives William a castle and a toy knight. The toy knight comes to life and tells William about a necklace that can be used to shrink people. William decides to shrink Mrs. Phillips but then regrets his decision. The only way for William to make things right is to shrink himself and join the Silver Knight on a quest to defeat the evil wizard, Alastor. William shows bravery by defeating Alastor all by himself. He then returns to the real world and restores Mrs. Phillips to her normal size. In the end, William learns that he is old enough and brave enough to take care of himself. As you can see, this story is full of suspense!

Mini-Lessons

In these lessons...your students will be practicing expository writing. Students will work on a formal writing project that requires them to go through all phases of the writing process. Documents are given in this lesson to help your students organize and draft their writing. However, you will need to use your own resources for teaching the other phases of the writing process. You will need at least five days for this project.

Suggested Lesson Sequence:
- Day 1 – Draft
- Day 2 – Continue drafting
- Day 3 – Revise
- Day 3 – Edit and begin publishing
- Day 4 – Continue publishing
- Day 5 – Share
- Day 6 – Share

Students will use the drafting organizer as a scaffold for their first drafts.

Learning Targets:

Write an expository piece (W 2)
- **Literary essay**

Write clearly and coherently for task and audience (W 4)

Practice all stages of the writing process, including publishing (W 5, 6)

Recall information and experiences to build and present knowledge (W 8, 9)

Write for an extended period of time (W 10)

Apply and use key vocabulary (L 6)

Present ideas (SL 4, 6)

Connect:

We have been learning…
…that good readers write in order to monitor their comprehension while reading and get to deeper thinking. We have also learned that readers write in order to synthesize and reflect on their thinking.

Teach:

Today I am going to teach you…

…that good readers write in order to share their thinking about a book with someone else. Today we will be starting a formal writing project. We will be writing literary essays in response to the book *The Castle in the Attic.*

We will be using the following prompt for our essays:

Prove how the Code of Chivalry helped William overcome tests and prove his goodness. Describe how the Code of Chivalry has helped you overcome tests or will help you overcome tests in your own life.

For our formal writing, we will be working outside of the reader's notebook. We will need to use loose-leaf paper as we go through all stages of the writing process:
- Pre-writing
- Drafting
- Revising
- Editing
- Publishing
- Sharing

Introduce and hand out the draft sheet.

Scaffold:

(Depending on your students' levels of readiness, you will need to decide whether the assignment will be done as :
- Shared writing—written as a group on chart paper or a document camera while students copy this writing into their reader's notebooks.
- Guided writing—started as a group on chart paper or a document camera and then released to be completed collaboratively or independently.
- Collaborative writing—each student works collaboratively with a partner, but is responsible for his or her own writing.
- Independent writing—completed by the student with limited or no guidance.)

Share Out:

After students complete their writing, have them share their essays with partners or the class. If this were set up as a formal presentation with media support, this activity would meet the requirements of SL 5.

Code of Chivalry

Compassionate
Someone who is compassionate helps others who are in need.

Honest
An honest person tells the truth and believes in the truth.

Strong
True strength comes from inside you when you believe in yourself.

Brave
Being brave means doing what is right, even when it takes courage.

Forgiving
Someone who shows forgiveness will be kind to his or her enemies.

Loyal
A person is loyal when they stay true to their closest friends.

On William's quest to get the necklace from the evil wizard Alastor, he used the Code of Chivalry to overcome many tests. William used _____, _____ and _____. I can/will use these same knightly characteristics to overcome tests in my life.

RULE OF CHIVALRY	WILLIAM	MYSELF
Definition:	First, William showed _____ when he…	I have shown/will show _____ when/if…
Definition:	Second, William showed _____ when he…	I have shown/will show _____ when/if…
Definition:	Third, William showed _____ when he…	I have shown/will show _____ when/if…

In conclusion the rules of chivalry helped William_____.
They also help / will help me_____.

The Castle in the Attic Unit of Study

Codes of Chivalry

On William's quest to get the necklace from the evil wizard Alastar, he used the code of chivalry to overcome many tests. William used strength, bravery and loyalty.

First William showed bravery when he goes through the forest alone and faces the dragon. Bravery means doing what is right even when it takes courage. I showed bravery when I stood up to a fight. It took a lot of courage in me to say stop.

Second William showed strength when he goes through the forest alone and faces the dragon. Strength means when true strength comes from inside you when you believe in yourself. I showed strength by adding fractions in math class. It took a lot of listening and focusing to do fractions.

Third William showed loyalty. He showed loyalty by risking his life to save Mrs. Phillips. A person is loyal when they stay true to their closest friends. I showed loyalty when I stood up for my friends. It took loyalty to be on their side.

In conclusion the rules of chivalry helped William defeat Alastair and turn him into led. They also helped me learn the code of chivalry.

Victoria

1-17-11

References

Angelillo, J. (2003). *Writing about reading: From book talk to literary essays, grades 3–8.* Portsmouth, NH: Heinemann.

Auman, M. (2010). *Step up to writing curriculum.* Longmount, CO: Sopris West.

Buckner, A. (2009). *Notebook connections: Strategies for the reader's notebook.* Portland, ME: Stenhouse.

Calkins, L. (2001). *The art of teaching reading.* New York, NY: Longman.

Common Core State Standards Initiative. (2010). *Common Core State Standards for English language arts & literacy in history/social studies, science and technical subjects, appendix A.* Washington, DC: Author.

Cunningham, P. M., & Allington, R. L. (2007). *Classrooms that work: They can all read and write.* Boston, MA: Pearson Education Inc.

Schmoker, M. (1996). *Write more, grade less.* Retrieved June 2, 2011 from www.mikeschmoker.com/write-more.html

Schmoker, M. (2011). *Focus.* Alexandria, VA: Association for Supervision & Curriculum Development.

Taberski, S. (2000). *On solid ground: Strategies for teaching reading, K–3.* Portsmouth, NH: Heinemann.

Winthrop, E. (1985). *The castle in the attic.* New York, NY: Yearling.

Zemelman, S., Daniels, H., & Hyde, A. (2005). *Best practice: Today's standards for teaching and learning in America's schools.* Portsmouth, NH: Heinemann.

Vocabulary Handbook

The Castle in the Attic
by Elizabeth Winthrop

Name: _____

WORD PART		MEANING	PART OF SPEECH
a-	prefix	from, away	
-able	suffix	able to, can be done	adjective
ad-	prefix	to, toward	
-age	suffix		noun
-al	suffix		noun or adjective
-ant	suffix	person who	noun
ap-	prefix	to, toward	
apt	root	fitted to, joined	
-ate	suffix		adjective
capt (cap, ceit, cept)	root	catch, seize, take hold of	
ceit (cap, capt, cept)	root	catch, seize, take hold of	
com-	prefix	together, with	
con-	prefix	with	
cour (cor, cord)	root	heart	
cur	root	to give attention to, to take care of	
de-	prefix	not; away from	
dign	root	worthy of respect or honor	
dis-	prefix	separate; not	
dit	root	give	
-dom	suffix		noun
domit	root	tame, subdued	
dur (dura, duro)	root	hard, tough, lasting	
-ed	suffix		past tense verb adjective
-ede	suffix		noun
-eer	suffix	someone who	noun
emi (ami, amic)	root	friend	
en-	prefix	inward; to cause to be; not	
-er	suffix	someone who	noun
-ess	suffix	female	noun
ex-	prefix	out, out from, away	
fac	root	to make, to do, to cause	
fer	root	to carry, to bring	
flux	root	flow, smooth movement	
forc (fort)	root	power, strength	
fortun (fortu)	root	luck	

The Castle in the Attic Unit of Study

-ful	suffix	full of	adjective
-fy	suffix	make, do, cause	verb
harmon	root	fitting together, agreement	
honor (hono, honest)	root	honor, honesty	
-ia	suffix		noun
-ible	suffix	able to, can be done	adjective
-ic	suffix		adjective
-ice	suffix		noun
im- (in-)	prefix	in, into, inside; not	
in- (im-)	prefix	in, into, inside; not	
-ing	suffix		present tense verb
inter-	prefix	between, among, together	
-ious	suffix		adjective
ir-	prefix	not	
-ish	suffix	characteristic of, like	adjective
-ism	suffix	belief in, practice of	noun
-ist	suffix	someone who believes in	noun
-ity	suffix		noun
-ive	suffix		adjective
-less	suffix	lacking, without	adjective
memor	root	remember	
-ment	suffix		noun
migr	root	to move, wander	
mis-	prefix	bad, harsh, wrong	
mis	root	send, to cause to go	
motive (mot, mov)	root	move, motion	
nat	root	born, birth	
-ness	suffix		noun
not	root	to know, notice, recognize	
of- (ob-)	prefix	toward, before	
omen (omin)	root	foreboding, believed to indicate evil	
optim	root	best, exceptionally good	
-or	suffix	someone who	noun
ordi	root	to begin; order	
-ous	suffix		adjective
pact (pac, peac, peas)	root	peace, eased anger	

pari	root	to come into sight, visible	
pass	root	feeling	
pedi (ped, pio)	root	foot	
pio (ped, pedi)	root	foot	
point	root	punch, pierce, point, sting	
posit	root	placement, positioning	
prim (prin)	root	first, chief	
prin (prim)	root	first, chief	
pro-	prefix	before, place before	
prov	root	upright, good, honest	
quest	root	to seek, to ask	
re-	prefix	again	
-s	suffix	more than one	plural noun
sacr (sacro)	root	sacred, holy, religious	
silen	root	absence of sound, quiet	
-sion	suffix		noun
sol (soli)	root	alone, only	
spir (spira)	root	breath of life, spirit, soul	
spons	root	promise	
talis (teleo)	combining form	end, result, fulfillment	
tempt	root	to influence, to test	
tense	root	stretched, strained, taut	
termin	root	end, last, final	
-tion	suffix		noun
tra (treat)	root	draw together	
treacher	root	deceiver, trickster	
tyrann	root	absolute ruler, oppressor	
un-	prefix	not	
uni	root	one, single	
val (valid, vail, vale)	root	to be worth, to be strong	
vance	root	move forward	
vers	root	bend, turn	
-y	suffix		adjective

Vocabulary: Making Connections

Target Word:

quest

Context:

"…suddenly William is off on a fantastic <u>quest</u> to another land and another time—
where a fiery dragon and an evil wizard are waiting to do battle…" (blurb).

What it is…   **What it is not…**

_____   _____

_____   _____

_____   _____

I'd probably find this word in these contexts (places, events, people, situations):

Text to World

I'll remember this word by connecting it to:

(word, phrase, sketch)

Vocabulary: Contrasts

In epic fantasy novels, there will always be a hero and a villain.

Target Words:

hero vs. villain

What it is…

_____

_____

_____

_____

What it is…

_____

_____

_____

_____

I'll remember this word by:

I'll remember this word by:

Vocabulary: Making Connections

Target Word:
deceitful

Context:

"On Saturday morning, William took [the picture of Mrs. Phillips's husband and her mother's pearl circle pin] and hid them in the shoebox that held his rock collection" (Inferred on pp. 4 & 5).

William lies when his mother asks him if he's seen Mrs. Phillips's things (Inferred on p. 6).

What it is...   **What it is not...**

_____   _____

_____   _____

_____   _____

_____   _____

I'd probably find this word in these contexts (places, events, people, situations):

Text to World

I'll remember this word by connecting it to:

(word, phrase, sketch)

Vocabulary: Making Connections

Target Word:
chivalry

Context:

"You have the kind of gentle soul that accepts the rules of <u>chivalry</u>. If you hadn't turned out the way you did, William, I would never have entrusted the castle to you" (p. 9).

What it is...   **What it is not...**

_____   _____

_____   _____

_____   _____

_____   _____

I'd probably find this word in these contexts (places, events, people, situations):

Text to World

```



```

I'll remember this word by connecting it to:

(word, phrase, sketch)

```



```

Vocabulary: Making Connections

Target Word:

tradition

Context:

"It's a family <u>tradition</u>. You're supposed to meet the Silver Knight on your own. My father made me do it that way…" (p. 13).

What it is…   **What it is not…**

_____   _____

_____   _____

_____   _____

_____

I'd probably find this word in these contexts (places, events, people, situations):

Text to World

```
┌─────────────────────────────────────────────────┐
│                                                   │
│                                                   │
│                                                   │
│                                                   │
└─────────────────────────────────────────────────┘
```

I'll remember this word by connecting it to:

(word, phrase, sketch)

```
┌─────────────────────────────────────────────────┐
│                                                   │
│                                                   │
│                                                   │
└─────────────────────────────────────────────────┘
```

Vocabulary: Contrasts

Context:

"Are you <u>friend</u> or <u>foe</u>? I am not frightened by your size, my good sir, and I will fight you with every ounce of strength left in me, if that be your wish" (p. 21).

Target Words:
friend vs. foe

What it is...   **What it is...**

_____   _____

_____   _____

_____   _____

_____   _____

I'll remember this word by: **I'll remember this word by:**

Vocabulary: Making Connections

Target Word:

power

Context:

"I sensed, even then, [Alastor's] desperate need to control people, to have <u>power</u>" (p. 33).

What it is...

_____

_____

_____

_____

What it is not...

_____

_____

_____

_____

I'd probably find this word in these contexts (places, events, people, situations):

Text to World

```



```

I'll remember this word by connecting it to:

(word, phrase, sketch)

```



```

Vocabulary: Making Connections

Target Word:

legend

Context:

"He never talked to me all those years I played with him. There was that <u>legend</u> about him.
Maybe it's the same one the Silver Knight told you" (p. 48).

What it is...   **What it is not...**

_____   _____

_____   _____

_____   _____

_____   _____

I'd probably find this word in these contexts (places, events, people, situations):

Text to World

```
┌────────────────────────────────────────────────────────┐
│                                                          │
│                                                          │
│                                                          │
│                                                          │
└────────────────────────────────────────────────────────┘
```

I'll remember this word by connecting it to:

(word, phrase, sketch)

```
┌────────────────────────────────────────────────────────┐
│                                                          │
│                                                          │
│                                                          │
│                                                          │
└────────────────────────────────────────────────────────┘
```

Vocabulary: Contrasts

Context:

"Alastor controlled my father's every action" (Tyranny inferred on p. 36).

"I shall be going back to reclaim my kingdom from Alastor" (Freedom inferred on p. 51).

Target Words:

freedom vs. tyranny

What it is…

_____

_____

_____

_____

What it is…

_____

_____

_____

_____

I'll remember this word by:

I'll remember this word by:

Vocabulary: Making Connections

Target Word:

unwilling

Context:

William is <u>unwilling</u> to let Mrs. Phillips leave.

What it is...

_____

_____

_____

_____

What it is not...

_____

_____

_____

_____

I'd probably find this word in these contexts (places, events, people, situations):

Text to World

I'll remember this word by connecting it to:

(word, phrase, sketch)

Vocabulary: Making Connections

Target Word:

disapproval

Context:

"My father would be furious if he knew there was a fire going in the attic" (Inferred on p. 58).

"…he knew underneath he could not face her <u>disapproval</u> again" (p. 77).

What it is…

_____

_____

_____

_____

What it is not…

_____

_____

_____

_____

I'd probably find this word in these contexts (places, events, people, situations):

Text to World

I'll remember this word by connecting it to:

(word, phrase, sketch)

Vocabulary: Making Connections

Target Word:

regret

Context:

"…I know I made a mistake" (Inferred on p. 96).

What it is…

_____

_____

_____

_____

What it is not…

_____

_____

_____

_____

I'd probably find this word in these contexts (places, events, people, situations):

Text to World

[ ]

I'll remember this word by connecting it to:

(word, phrase, sketch)

[ ]

Vocabulary: Making Connections

Target Word:

peace offering

Context:

"When he'd finally assembled everything on the bed it looked like a very odd assortment. One recorder, one bear, one box of candles, one toothbrush, one jar of marmite (as a <u>peace offering</u> to Mrs. Phillips)..." (p. 88).

What it is...   **What it is not...**

_____   _____

_____   _____

_____   _____

_____   _____

I'd probably find this word in these contexts (places, events, people, situations):

Text to World

I'll remember this word by connecting it to:

(word, phrase, sketch)

Vocabulary: Making Connections

Target Word:

mercy

Context:

"Never kill a foe who is begging for <u>mercy</u>" (p. 98).

What it is...   **What it is not...**

_____   _____

_____   _____

_____   _____

_____   _____

I'd probably find this word in these contexts (places, events, people, situations):

Text to World

```
┌─────────────────────────────────────────────┐
│                                               │
│                                               │
│                                               │
│                                               │
└─────────────────────────────────────────────┘
```

I'll remember this word by connecting it to:

(word, phrase, sketch)

```
┌─────────────────────────────────────────────┐
│                                               │
│                                               │
│                                               │
│                                               │
└─────────────────────────────────────────────┘
```

Vocabulary: Making Connections

Target Word:

knight

Context:

"And whatever happens you must remember one thing…that you have within your heart the weapons you need. The heart and soul of a <u>knight</u> in the body of a squire" (p. 104).

What it is…   **What it is not…**

_____   _____

_____   _____

_____   _____

_____

I'd probably find this word in these contexts (places, events, people, situations):

Text to World

I'll remember this word by connecting it to:

(word, phrase, sketch)

Vocabulary: Making Connections

Target Word:

tempted

Context:

"Strange apparitions will <u>tempt</u> you on every side, but no matter what,
you must stay on the path" (p. 111).

"…he didn't dare look too closely in case he was being <u>tempted</u> again" (p. 116).

What it is…   **What it is not…**

_____   _____

_____   _____

_____   _____

_____   _____

I'd probably find this word in these contexts (places, events, people, situations):

Text to World

I'll remember this word by connecting it to:

(word, phrase, sketch)

Vocabulary: Making Connections

Target Word:

apparition

Context:

"Strange <u>apparitions</u> will tempt you on every side, but no matter what,
you must stay on the path" (p. 111).

What it is…

_____

_____

_____

_____

What it is not…

_____

_____

_____

I'd probably find this word in these contexts (places, events, people, situations):

Text to World

I'll remember this word by connecting it to:

(word, phrase, sketch)

Vocabulary: Making Connections

Target Word:

steadfast

Context:

"[William] wanted to reach the castle that day, if possible, and he didn't want to hear any more terrible stories about the power of the wizard" (Inferred on pp. 121 & 122).

What it is...

_____

_____

_____

_____

What it is not...

_____

_____

_____

_____

I'd probably find this word in these contexts (places, events, people, situations):

Text to World

\
\
\
\
\

I'll remember this word by connecting it to:

(word, phrase, sketch)

\
\
\
\
\

The Castle in the Attic Unit of Study

Vocabulary: Making Connections

Target Word:

compassionate

Context:

"Be compassionate to the needy" (p. 122).

What it is...

_____

_____

_____

_____

What it is not...

_____

_____

_____

_____

I'd probably find this word in these contexts (places, events, people, situations):

Text to World

```



```

I'll remember this word by connecting it to:

(word, phrase, sketch)

```



```

Vocabulary: Contrasts

Context:

"You must give up this <u>foolish</u> plan. Nobody can pass into the castle without Alastor's permission" (p. 128).

Target Words:

foolish vs. wise

What it is…

_____

_____

_____

_____

What it is…

_____

_____

_____

_____

I'll remember this word by:

I'll remember this word by:

Vocabulary: Making Connections

Target Word:

courage

Context:

"He was terrified…[He] faced the beast head on. The dragon looked stunned by the arrival of a rather small, not very well armed opponent…" (Inferred on p. 135).

What it is…   **What it is not…**

_____   _____

_____   _____

_____   _____

_____   _____

I'd probably find this word in these contexts (places, events, people, situations):

Text to World

I'll remember this word by connecting it to:

(word, phrase, sketch)

Vocabulary: Contrasts

Context:

"This time there were no scenes of fiery horror but only the terrified and lonely eyes of the cat <u>imprisoned</u> inside this grotesque green body" (p. 138).

Target Words:

imprisoned vs. freed

What it is…

_____

_____

_____

_____

What it is…

_____

_____

_____

_____

I'll remember this word by:

I'll remember this word by:

The Castle in the Attic Highlighting Directions and Labels for the Instructor's Book

The following pages consist of labels and directions for labeling and highlighting the teacher's copy of *The Castle in the Attic*. Some teachers may find these highlights and labels helpful when conducting lessons. Begin by putting the labels in the book, then highlight.

To print the labels, use clear full-sheet labels, such as Avery #18655. Cut the labels once they have been printed. Then, follow the directions given below to insert labels into your book.

I suggest using gel highlighters for highlighting, because they will not bleed to the other side of the page. You will need a pink, a yellow, and an orange highlighter.

THE CASTLE IN THE ATTIC HIGHLIGHTING DIRECTIONS FOR THE INSTRUCTOR'S BOOK

Pink = Teacher Modeling	Yellow = Turn & Talk	Orange = Vocabulary
Color	**Book starts on p. 3 (Yearling)**	**Word or sentence**
Pink	4	He ran out of the room before she could say anything else.
Yellow	5	He knew Mrs. Phillips would never leave without them.
Yellow	6	"I think she'd even leave her picture behind if she had to."
Yellow	7	"And I'm not going to say one more word about it."
Orange	9	chivalry
Pink	10	The metal grille disappeared into the wall above.
Yellow	11	Up above, William could just see the minstrels' gallery, where troubadours and jesters sang to entertain the lords and ladies dining below.
Yellow	12	"I knew you'd like it."
Line	12	next to "Are there any knights?"
Orange	13	tradition
Pink	13	"The castle's really wonderful," he said again.
Yellow	15	"But the whole time I played with the castle, he was stiff and cold as lead."
Yellow	16	He went upstairs to do his homework.
Pink	18	The smell of her perfume hung in the air after she'd left.
Orange	21	friend
Orange	21	foe
Yellow	21	He was being threatened by a seated miniature man waving a pin-sized knife!

The Castle in the Attic Unit of Study

Yellow	25	William fell asleep with his thumb rubbing the small pinprick the dagger had made in his palm.
Pink	27	William slid a piece of toast and half a slice of bacon into his napkin and tucked them up his shirt-sleeve.
Yellow	28	Nobody else in their class ever got to school early.
Yellow	30	Everything about her made him feel safe and happy.
Pink	30 & 31	He was so distracted by these thoughts that he almost tripped over the castle.
Line	31	next to "Young man, hold up, hold up…"
Pink	32	"…they took their time considering the matter of the disease and conferring with one another."
Yellow	33	"…but I sensed even then his desperate need to control people, to have power."
Yellow	34	"…but I never learned much more about it because after a while he grew secretive around me."
Yellow	35	"Alastor was poisoning his mind and his body at the same time."
Yellow	36	Sir Simon stopped speaking and covered his face for a moment.
Yellow	38	"I am not small in my own country, young man, only in yours."
Line	38	near "The Silver Knight patted the pouch…"
Pink	40	"I'll catch a bug tomorrow," William added as he went down the stairs.
Yellow	42	"It's more fun than practicing the piano."
Yellow	45	"Banging the wall seems to help," he said as he flipped the switch.
Yellow	46	I wouldn't feel this way if she hadn't decided to leave.

Pink = Teacher Modeling	Yellow = Turn & Talk	Orange = Vocabulary
Color	**Book starts on p. 3 (Yearling)**	**Word or sentence**
Orange	48	legend
Yellow	48	They said no more about the Silver Knight.
Pink	53	He seemed so sure of himself that William was reluctant to tell him it was impossible.
Yellow	53	"Until then, I shall prepare myself."
Yellow	56	"I was just kidding."
Pink	59	But now you're going away, he thought, and that makes everything different.
Orange	60	approval
Yellow	61	"I don't think you'll believe that until I leave."
Yellow	62	Of course, he could. With the token.
Line	62	next to "All that day, and the next…"
Pink	63	He would worry about that later.
Parentheses	63	Put parentheses around ("As Alastor once told me…I will protect her from harm.")
Orange	63	willingly
Orange	63	unwillingly
Yellow	64	He must not let anything change that.
Yellow	66	"Then don't blame me for what happens," he said as he left.
Yellow	68	"Now give me a big hug and go back in the house."
Yellow	70	"I want you both back up to the attic before anything else happens."

Pink	72	…he could see she was disappointed by the curve of her shoulders.
Yellow	73	It made him feel oddly lonely.
Yellow	75	"It's too dark and creepy up here."
Orange	77	disapproval
Yellow	77	…pushed comfortingly against the lump in his stomach.
Pink	80	"Every day she spends here, she loses time in her own world."
Yellow	83	"…I must have decided to go," he said to the empty room.
Yellow	87	They stood there a moment longer without speaking.
Line	87	next to "When William sneaked up later…"
Pink	88	But he knew it was a promise nobody could make to him.
Orange	88	Peace offering
Yellow	90	…his bike leaned against his hip, staring after him.
Yellow	92	"Enter, young William," was all he said.
Pink	96	"The half that sets us free."
Orange	96	free
Yellow	97	"Tomorrow, my boy, your training begins in earnest."
Orange	98	mercy
Yellow	98	"As you wish, my lady."
Yellow	101	"Another weapon. You get back on your feet a little faster that way."
Line	102	next to "At the end of the week…"

Pink = Teacher Modeling	Yellow = Turn & Talk	Orange = Vocabulary
Color	**Book starts on p. 3 (Yearling)**	**Word or sentence**
Pink	103	"There are rules in the world of magic just as there are in our world."
Yellow	104	What would he meet?
Orange	104	knight
Yellow	107	When he glanced back the second time, the drawbridge had been raised.
Pink	109	"It can be," was all the knight replied.
Yellow	110	…birds were passing word of their progress along to someone ahead.
Orange	110	apparitions
Orange	111	tempt
Yellow	111	He was pleased that his voice sounded stronger than he felt.
Line	111	next to "They set off again…"
Pink	112	…darkness had closed down around them again.
Yellow	113	…he sank to the ground and cried until he fell asleep.
Orange	116	tempted
Yellow	116	…the road led him out into the middle of a large field.
Line	116	next to "William slipped his recorder into his pouch…"
Pink	118	"They say everybody is Alastor's spy."
Yellow	120	…a few ears of corn and some stunted grain grew in the dry brown fields.
Yellow	121	The water tasted brackish, and he took only enough to wet his mouth.

Line	121	next to "He knew by the position of the sun…"
Orange	122	compassionate
Pink	122	"How can I help you?"
Yellow	124	Don't stray off the path.
Yellow	126	"I have been imprisoned inside that old man's shape for years."
Orange	126	imprisoned
Orange	128	foolish
Orange	128	fool
Yellow	128	"Perhaps that will help get me into the castle."
Line	128	next to "In some ways, you are quite the fool…"
Orange	128	fool
Pink	128	"But I will tell you what I know."
Yellow	129	"He told me that his grandmother was the Silver Knight's nurse."
Yellow	130	And he stood there waving until William turned the corner.
Pink	132	… right out of his mind and left it sitting there on the side of the road.
Yellow	133	Once he started walking toward the dragon, there would be no turning back.
Yellow	137	William sank to his knees in the dirt and let the recorder drop from his mouth.
Orange	138	imprisoned
Yellow	139	…across the drawbridge right up to the door and knocked loudly three times.
Pink	144	"No, sir," William ventured warily.
Yellow	146	How was he ever going to do that?
Yellow	148	…using it for a pillow, he went to sleep.

THE CASTLE IN THE ATTIC LABEL INSERT DIRECTIONS FOR THE INSTRUCTOR'S BOOK

Item	Book starts on p. 1 (Yearling)	Near sentence in book
Day 3	3	Top of chapter 1
Deceitful	5	Near "On Saturday morning, William took them…"
Deceitful	6	Near "No, said William."
Day 4	8	Top of chapter 2
Day 6	12	Near "Are there any knights?"
Day 7	17	Top of chapter 3
Day 8	26	Top of chapter 4
Day 9	31	Near "Young man, hold up, hold up…"
Tyranny	36	Near "Alastor had put some sort of spell on the forest…"
Day 11	38	Near "The Silver Knight patted the pouch that hung…"
Day 12	49	Top of chapter 6
Freedom	53	Near "I shall be going back to reclaim my kingdom…"
Day 13	57	Top of chapter 7
Disapproval	58	Near "My father would be furious if he knew…"
Day 14	62	Near "All that day and the next…"
Day 14	63	Near "As Alastor once told me…"
Day 16	71	Top of chapter 8
Day 17	78	Top of chapter 9
Day 19	87	Near "When William sneaked up later to see…"
Day 21	93	Top of chapter 10
Regret	96	Near "Because I know I made a mistake…"

The Castle in the Attic Unit of Study

Day 22	102	Near "At the end of the week, Sir Simon declared…"
Day 23	108	Top of chapter 11
Day 24	111	Near "They set off again, more slowly this time."
Day 25	116	Near "William slipped his recorder into his pouch…"
Day 26	121	Near "He knew by the position of the sun…"
Steadfast	121	Near "He wanted to reach the castle that day if possible…"
Day 27	128	Near "In some ways, you are quite the fool…"
Day 28	131	Top of chapter 13
Courage	135	side of page
Steadfast	137	Near "He put the recorder back to his lips…"
Day 30	140	Top of chapter 14
Day 31	149	Top of chapter 15

Day 3—Good readers use comprehension strategies to identify important characters and infer character traits.

Day 4—Good readers pay attention to the setting of the story.

Day 6—Good readers recognize foreshadowing and stop to make predictions.

Day 7—Good readers use comprehension strategies to identify important characters and infer character traits.

Day 8—Good readers think about the main character's actions, words, and feelings in order to infer character traits.

Day 9—Good readers think about what events are important, as they read.

Day 11—Good readers consider the issues or conflicts within the story and think about how they are important.

Day 12—Good readers notice important information and use that important information to make predictions.

Day 13—Good readers continue to think about the problem in the story and consider how a character plans to solve the problem.

Day 14—Good readers compare characters when reading, and think about how those characters are similar or different.

Day 14—Good readers pay attention to the function of time when reading fantasy.

Day 16—Good readers infer the characters' feelings while reading.

Day 17—Good readers infer the main character's feelings and think about what motivates him or her to do things.

Day 19—Good readers make predictions based on what they know about the genre.

Day 21—Good readers continue to collect evidence to support a line of thinking while reading.

Day 22—Good readers notice how the author uses more than one plot to tell the story.

Day 23—Good readers sketch a map of the setting as they read to help them visualize where and when the story takes place.

Day 24—Good readers continue to collect evidence to support a line of thinking while reading.

Day 25—Good readers use the setting map to think about cause and effect.

Day 26—Good readers continue to collect evidence to support a line of thinking while reading.

Day 27—Good readers keep track of important characters in the second plot in order to monitor their comprehension while reading.

Day 28—Good readers, as they approach the end of the third quadrant of the book, look for the turning point in the story.

Day 30—Good readers make predictions about how the book will end based on the turning point.

Day 31(Read-In)—Good readers, once they reach the turning point, read without interruption to the end, in order to finish the book with enjoyment.

deceitful   tyranny   disapproval

deceitful   freedom   regret

steadfast   steadfast   courage